The Wreck of the *America*
in Southern Illinois

T0308074

The Wreck of the

America

in Southern Illinois

A Flatboat on the Ohio River

MARK J. WAGNER

Southern Illinois University Press • Carbondale

Copyright © 2015 by the Board of Trustees,
Southern Illinois University
All rights reserved
Printed in the United States of America

18 17 16 15   4 3 2 1

Cover illustrations: (*top*) Nineteenth-century
emigrant, or family, flatboat. *Bryant 1972.*
(*bottom*) The *America*, August 2002.

Library of Congress Cataloging-in-Publication Data
Wagner, Mark J.
The wreck of the "America" in southern Illinois :
a flatboat on the Ohio River / Mark J. Wagner.
pages cm
Summary: "The discovery of the wreck of what is probably an
early nineteenth-century flatboat in the bed of the Ohio River,
the research conducted at the wreck site, and the possible
causes of its sinking are described. Not a single intact original
example of the flatboat vessel type has been known to exist.
While the wreck is not completely intact, it provides new
information about this boat form"— Provided by publisher.
Includes bibliographical references.
ISBN 978-0-8093-3436-0 (paperback)
ISBN 0-8093-3436-4 (paperback)
ISBN 978-0-8093-3437-7 (e-book)
1. Flatboats—Ohio River—History.
2. Ohio River Valley—Antiquities
3. Excavations (Archaeology)—Ohio River Valley.
I. America (Flatboat) II. Title.
F518.W16 2015
977'.01—dc23   2015009460
Printed on recycled paper. ♻
The paper used in this publication meets the minimum
requirements of American National Standard for Information
Sciences—Permanence of Paper for Printed Library Materials,
ANSI Z39.48-1992. ∞

Perhaps no other craft that ever moved on land or sea provided such epi-sodes and contrasts, such diverse pictures of tragedy and revel as did the *flatboats* in which the vast host of floating pilgrims traveled the interior rivers of America . . . probably a million people lived in them for weeks at a time, during journeys of from three hundred to two thousand miles. They were built by the tens of thousands, *yet not one of them remains.* . . . [T]here is small chance for future Americans ever to see an example of the quaint boats into which men, women, children, horses, pigs, chickens, cows, dogs, kegs of powder, dishes, furniture, boxes of provisions, and farming implements were all loaded and jumbled together, to float down the rivers to somewhere.

—Dunbar, *A History of Travel in America*, volume 1, emphasis added

[W]e pass[ed] [in our Ohio River flatboat] on the right of Cash [*sic*] Island. . . . We had a narrow and somewhat difficult pass between two sand bars, the one lying on the right side of the Island and the other near the Indiana [Territory or Illinois] shore, the left bar appeared most dangerous *and had the wreck of a Boat lying upon it.*

—Anonymous, *The Journal of a Trip from Champaign County, Ohio, and down the Mississippi River to New Orleans with a Cargo of Flour, 25 Nov. 1805–26 July 1806*, emphasis added

Contents

Acknowledgments

$\mathcal{D}$ocumentation of the flatboat *America* could not have been completed without the assistance of a large number of volunteers. I particularly thank landowner Charles "Chuck" Kiestler and Pulaski County engineer Nick Niestrath. Both took a great interest in the project, helping staff and students from Southern Illinois University Carbondale (SIUC) in excavation and stabilization of the wreck whenever they could. I also acknowledge John Schwegman, the discoverer of the wreck in 2000 who helped during the 2002 investigations, for allowing us to analyze and photograph the artifacts that he and others recovered from the wreck in 2001. Other local residents I wish to thank include Monica Smith of the Cairo Public Library, who, with Chuck Kiestler, helped us coordinate our work at the wreck site, and Nancy Bush, who brought much appreciated refreshments to workers at the *America* site. Other volunteers include David Hart, the former owner of Egyptian Photo in Carbondale, who lent us wide-angle camera lenses with which to photograph the wreck. Others who assisted in documentation of the wreck include Mary R. McCorvie of the U.S. Department of Agriculture's Forest Service, and Nicola McCorvie Wagner.

Administrators and faculty members at SIUC who volunteered their time to help at the wreck site include John Haller, then the vice president of academic affairs, and assistant professor Robert Swenson of the Department of Architecture and Interior Design. I particularly thank Dr. Haller for his help at the *America* wreck site and his efforts at the time to locate a source of funding for the preservation and possible eventual display of this important aspect of the early history of southern Illinois. Bob Swenson also deserves many thanks for his interest and help throughout all aspects of this project, especially his assistance, along with that of his son Matt, in stabilizing the wreck in 2007, when the gunwale was in danger of washing away. Paul Welch of the Department of Anthropology used global-positioning-system equipment to provide us with a precise location of the wreck. Other university-affiliated volunteers who helped in the field documentation of the wreck included Bonnie Heidinger, Matt Lach, and SIUC anthropology students Jill Aud, Joel Aud, Erin Bilyeu, Brian Carlow, Candy Davis, Derek Kocher, Erinn Shockey, and Hilary Wheeler.

Various state and federal agency personnel helped in documentation of the *America*. Ann Haaker, the deputy state historic preservation officer, and chief staff archaeologist Joe Phillipe, both of the Illinois Historic Preservation Agency, were instrumental in providing funds from that agency. Don Ball and Jan Hemberger of the Louisville district office of the Corps of Engineers (COE) helped us secure federal permits. Terry Norris, a St. Louis district COE archaeologist, visited the wreck site early in the project and conclusively identified the wreck as an early 1800s flatboat. Finally, an earlier version of this book appeared as a rather lengthy article in the 2002 issue of *Illinois Archaeology*. I thank the current editor of the journal, Mike Conner, and the officers of the Illinois Archeological Survey board of directors for granting permission for us to republish much of the material that appeared in that article.

The Wreck of the *America*
in Southern Illinois

1. Introduction

*F*latboats represent one of the most common types of folk-built wooden vessels on the Ohio and Mississippi Rivers from the late eighteenth to the late nineteenth century. Referred to variously as "arks," "Kentucky boats," "New Orleans boats," "Mississippi boats," "broadhorns," and "hoop-pole boats," these flat-bottomed boats were the primary means by which local farmers and merchants shipped farm produce and goods to downriver markets. Emigrants also constructed flatboats to carry themselves and their families down the Ohio River to new homes in the west.

Government records indicate that thousands of flatboats descended the two rivers each year during the first decades of the nineteenth century. Although the exact number of this kind of boat built from the 1780s to the late 1800s is unknown, it almost certainly exceeded 100,000 vessels. Flatboats died out as a distinct vessel type along the Ohio River by the early 1900s, although the building of other flat-bottomed vessels continued. Not a single intact original example of the flatboat vessel type is known to exist today. As a result, our knowledge of the construction of these boats is based entirely on traveler's accounts, artist's illustrations, photographs, and memoirs collected from flatboat builders.

This situation changed in September 2000, when a group of local citizens discovered the partial remains of a flatboat approximately 1.5 miles (2.4 km) above Mound City along the Ohio River shoreline in Pulaski County, Illinois (Figure 1.1). The wreck was far down the bank, meaning it is completely exposed only during periods of extremely low water. John Schwegman, one of the discoverers of the wreck, received permission from the landowner to investigate it with the assistance of several volunteers. The recovered artifacts, which included clothing buttons, boat tools, and kitchen items, suggested the wreck dated to the latter part of the eighteenth or the early part of the nineteenth century. Schwegman concluded that the boat may

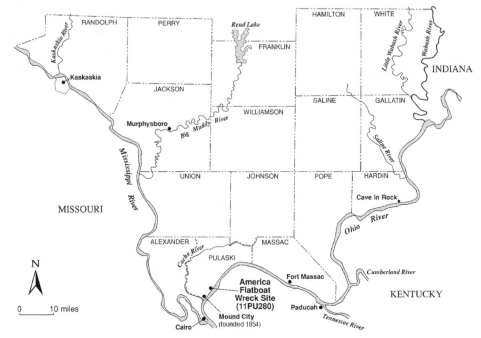

1.1. Location of the *America* wreck site in relation to early nineteenth-century towns and natural features in southern Illinois.

have been attacked and plundered by the notorious pirate Colonel Pfluger, or "Plug," who reportedly operated from the mouth of the nearby Cache River during the same period.[1]

Schwegman showed the silt-covered wreck site to archaeologists of Southern Illinois University Carbondale (SIUC) and the U.S. Army Corps of Engineers (COE) in summer 2001. The wreck, which was subsequently was named the *America* after a nearby town of the same name, was on the north, or Illinois, side of the river. Recognizing the importance of the wreck, the Illinois Historic Preservation Agency (IHPA) contracted with the Center for Archaeological Investigations (CAI) at SIUC in spring 2002 to conduct a detailed study of the *America*. The Louisville District Army COE, which has jurisdiction over the Ohio River shoreline, then issued a nationwide permit to SIUC for the archaeological investigations. Charles Kiestler, who owns the adjacent bank and shoreline, also granted permission for the investigations.

A team of CAI personnel (including myself), SIUC anthropology students, and university and local volunteers undertook documentation of the *America* in late summer 2002, when the Ohio River water level dropped low enough to once again expose the wreck (Figure 1.2). It became clear during the course of this fieldwork that the wreck was unstable and that part or all of the *America* could wash away downriver during the next rise of the Ohio River. Consequently, at the end of the investigations we covered the wreck with porous weed-guard fabric and filled the interior with gravel to hold the boat framework in place. This preservation procedure, as discussed in more detail in the last chapter of this book, is only a short-term solution; it is not clear how long the *America* will survive the strong currents associated with the yearly rises and falls of the Ohio River.

What We Did

We (CAI personnel at SIUC) developed a series of research questions regarding the type of vessel represented by the wreck, its age, and the techniques used in its construction prior to starting work at the wreck site. John Schwegman wrote a very good article that appeared in *Springhouse* magazine; in it he concluded that the wreck represented the remains of a late eighteenth- to early nineteenth-century flatboat that had sunk after being attacked by river pirates.[2] While his conclusion certainly was possible, we thought that further investigation of the wreck should be conducted

1.2. SIUC investigation of the *America* wreck site, summer 2002.

to determine exactly what sort of vessel it was and how it may have sunk. Flatboats were only one of a number of flat-bottomed types of vessel known to have been present on the Ohio River during the nineteenth century. As such, it was possible that the wreck represented the remains of another flat-bottomed vessel type such as a skiff or a houseboat rather than a flatboat. Second, although some of the artifacts recovered from the wreck may have been made during the eighteenth century, we believed that as a group they were more similar to artifact assemblages found at sites in southern Illinois that date to 1800–1830.[3] Third, it was our impression that the danger of river piracy along the lower Ohio River in the early 1800s had been greatly exaggerated by later writers.[4] We believed that the documentary record showed that flatboats faced a much greater danger than pirates, that is, sinking from natural causes such as succumbing to storms, hitting rocks and snags, and running aground.[5]

We used a combination of historical and archaeological research to address the above questions. We first defined the physical characteristics of the flatboat vessel type using information contained in eighteenth- and nineteenth-century descriptions of this vessel form. We then used first-hand accounts collected from nineteenth-century flatboat builders to obtain comparative information about the building techniques and structural elements characteristic of flatboats. We reviewed the history of navigation on the Ohio and Mississippi rivers to establish a historic context for the *America* wreck. Our review included an examination of the cultural and natural factors known to have resulted in flatboat wrecks. Our archaeological investigation of the wreck concentrated on documenting the *America* in detail through measurements, photography, and line drawings to recover information about its construction, its age, and the factors that may have led to its sinking. We then combined the results of the historic research, boat documentation, and artifact analyses to determine the vessel type, its age, its history, and possible causes of the wreck and abandonment of the *America*.

We concluded that the *America* did indeed represent the remains of an early 1800s flatboat that had been traveling down the Ohio River when it unexpectedly sank. Where it was coming from or where it was going are questions we will never be able to answer. But we were able to answer questions regarding how it had been built, which, as it turned out, was different in some regards from beliefs about the construction of such boats based on historic accounts. We also were able to determine the probable cause behind the sinking, which most likely was the failure of a rotting joint at the stern of the boat rather than any sort of violent attack. While not as romantic an ending as an attack by pirates, the fate of the *America*—that is, wrecking from natural causes and being stranded and abandoned on the shoreline of the Ohio River—was one suffered by thousands of other flatboats during the more than 100 years of the "flatboat era" (ca. 1770–1900), when these boats were the most frequently seen vessel type on either the Ohio or the Mississippi River.

2. Arks, Broadhorns, and Other Flat-Bottomed Boats

The building of flat-bottomed plank boats is one of the oldest boat-building traditions in the world, dating back at least 3,300 years ago in England.[1] An essential characteristic of flat-bottomed plank vessels is that they are *edge-joined* vessels. That is, the planks used in their construction join edge to edge rather than overlapping as in other wooden vessel types. Flat-bottomed plank boats also are, for the most part, *shell-built* boats. Such boats "were first thought of and visualized as a shell of wooden planks . . . conceived, designed, and built from the outside in."[2] In contrast to the edge-joined shell-built boat type is the non-edge-joined *skeleton-built* boat form. Skeleton-built boats, which are built from the inside out, are constructed around a wooden frame with the shape of the entire vessel determined by this preerected framework.[3] Examples of non-edge-joined skeleton-built boats include the large wooden sailing vessels such as schooners, brigs, and warships built in America and Europe throughout the seventeenth to nineteenth centuries.

Europeans who immigrated to North America appear to have introduced the flat-bottomed edge-joined boatbuilding tradition into both the southern and the northern colonies as early as the latter part of the seventeenth century. Newell cites one source that indicates vessels described as "flat bottomed pull boats" were in use in the southern colonies as early as 1638.[4] Flat-bottomed water craft also were in use on the waterways of northern colonies including Pennsylvania and Connecticut as early as 1685.[5] Only with the defeat of France and the ceding of the upper Ohio Valley to England at the end of the Seven Years War, however, did a need develop for larger flat-bottomed river craft capable of carrying large numbers of emigrants and their goods downriver. With the end of this war, thousands of English colonists began crossing over the Appalachian Mountains in search of new land in the upper Ohio Valley. By 1770 the flow of immigrants coming over the mountains had turned into a stream, and by 1780 all of the best lands in western Virginia and southwestern Pennsylvania already had been taken.[6] With the opening of the Northwest Territory (which included parts of present-day Illinois, Ohio, Indiana, Michigan, and Wisconsin) for settlement in 1787, the stream of immigrants across the mountains became a flood as "hundreds of thousands of the population began . . . [a] journey to the headwaters of the Ohio . . . [to] set up new homes in the forest."[7]

Ohio and Mississippi River Flatboats

The Ohio River represented a natural migration route for late eighteenth-century immigrants bound to the present-day states of Kentucky, Ohio, Indiana, and Illinois. It is also during this period that the term *flatboat* came into common use as a name for the large boxlike edge-joined flat-bottomed craft that became the predominant vessel type on the Ohio and Mississippi rivers prior to the Civil War. Flatboat travel down the Ohio appears to have begun in the 1770s with the defeat of the Shawnee in Lord Dunmore's War and the opening of Kentucky to Euro-American settlement.[8] Kentucky-bound settlers called the boats that they built to descend the Ohio River "Kentucky boats," "family boats," "broadhorns," and "arks," nicknames that indicated the destination of these boats as well as their purpose. Convoys of flatboats, sometimes carrying several hundred emigrants, descended the Ohio River carrying families, their goods, and their animals. The term *ark* was based on the resemblance of such boats, with their loads of animals and people, to the biblical Noah's Ark.

By the late 1780s, if not earlier, westbound emigrants could buy flatboats rather than having to construct such vessels themselves. In 1788 one Philadelphia newspaper advised travelers, "Boats of every dimension may be had at Elizabeth Town [on the Ohio River at] . . . short notice, and on as reasonable terms as at any place on said river."[9] Descending the Ohio River during the first 11 months of 1788 alone were more than 900 boats, most of which were bound for Kentucky.[10]

New Orleans became the natural market for Ohio Valley farmers and merchants who lived in areas that lacked the roads or canals needed to get their goods to market. Starting in 1806, if not earlier, inexperienced flatboat travelers could purchase an authoritative guide to the Ohio and Mississippi

Rivers called *The Navigator*. Written by Zadok Cramer of Pittsburgh, this small volume contained detailed instructions and charts of these two rivers. Cramer, who made at least one journey down these rivers himself, constantly revised this book throughout the 1820s with new information supplied to him by river travelers. In many cases Cramer's book, which was small enough to be carried in a large pocket or bag, was the only source of information about what lay ahead for a group of western-bound emigrants.

Flatboat cargoes consisted of every type of item produced in the Ohio and Mississippi valleys: flour, corn, wheat, potatoes, tobacco, fruit, whiskey, beans, onions, sauerkraut, and so on. Live animals, including horses, cattle, pigs, sheep, and chickens, also were carried downriver. Flatboats transported manufactured products, too, such as brooms, buckets, glass, farm machinery, lumber, and coal.[11] Hoop-pole boats carried hay bales, held in place by bent willow poles, down the Ohio River late into the nineteenth century.[12] Pre–Civil War flatboats from Kentucky also carried human cargoes in the form of African American slaves who were to be sold in the southern slave states that bordered the Mississippi River.[13] Shipping items downriver was an extremely risky financial venture but one to which farmers and merchants along the river had no alternative if they wished to get their produce to market. The first flatboats to reach New Orleans in any given year found ready buyers and could easily dispose of their goods and begin the journey home. Late arrivers found all the warehouses and ships in the city full and no takers for their cargo at any price. Before the Civil War, the southern Illinois merchant Daniel Harmon Brush declared the shipping of produce and other goods downriver to New Orleans on flatboats to be "not only hazardous, but unprofitable as well . . . [but] when taken in the stuff had to be disposed of, and to do that perilous ventures must be undertaken."[14]

• • •

Flatboat travel along the Ohio increased markedly after the opening of the Spanish-held port of New Orleans to American commerce in the late eighteenth century.[15] In 1807 a total of 1,223 flatboats arrived in New Orleans.[16] A few years later almost 1,000 flatboats passed Louisville, Kentucky, on their way to the Mississippi River valley.[17] In 1832 the Corps of Engineers estimated that more than 4,000 flatboats had descended the Mississippi River that year alone. In 1845–1846, approximately 3,000 flatboats were recorded as having reached New Orleans, but this is believed to be less than the actual number, as many boats went unrecorded or sold out their produce before reaching New Orleans. In 1847 a reported 3,336 flatboats docked at Cincinnati, Ohio, 700 of which continued farther downriver. By the 1850s the number had increased to 6,000. As late as 1853, flatboats still carried one-fourth of all flour, one-seventh of all whiskey, and two-thirds of the pork and bacon produced in Cincinnati despite competition from steamboats.[18] Flatboat traffic declined steadily in importance as a means to transport goods to market after the Civil War, due to competition from railroads as well as decreased insurance rates that lowered the price of shipping on steamboats. Many farmers and local businessmen, however, still found it cheaper during this time to ship goods downriver on flatboats they built themselves in which their only investments were time and labor and possibly the cost of the wood than to pay the freight costs charged by railroads and steamboats. As late as 1878 Captain "Bigger" P. McFarlan of Elizabethtown, Illinois, shipped "100,000 poles and 9,000 [barrel] staves" down the Ohio River on a flatboat.[19] Three years later one of McFarlan's hoop-pole boats sank after it struck a snag about 100 miles above New Orleans. The final death knell to the Ohio River flatboats came in the late 1800s with the construction of locks and dams on the river. Navigators of flatboats, unwieldy craft at the best of times, found it extremely difficult to pass through the same locks that steam-powered vessels could navigate with ease.

What Is a Flatboat?

Ohio and Mississippi River flatboats shared physical characteristics that distinguished them from other late eighteenth-century Ohio River vessels such as the keelboat. These traits included the use of chine-girder construction in the shaping of the gunwales that formed the two long sides of the boat bottom, a flat edge-joined plank bottom, and edge-joined plank sides that varied in height from four to six feet. Chine-girder construction describes the technique whereby a single log is split in half to create two equal-sized timbers or girders (see this book's appendix for definitions of this and other boat-related terms).[20] Nineteenth-century flatboat builders throughout the Ohio River valley consistently referred to these girders as "gunwales,"[21] and I follow this usage throughout this report. The inboard sides of the bottoms of the two gunwales were rabbeted to create a ledge that held the ends of the floor planks. The rabbet was cut to the same depth as the thickness of the plank, creating a smooth bottom from one side of the boat to the other. Stanchions, or wooden uprights, were set into the gunwales and end girders to construct a framework to which the planks forming the sides of the boat were attached using wooden treenails (i.e., pegs). The planks were pegged end to end in strakes (i.e., rows) to form the sides and ends of the boat. The stern and sides of the flatboat hull consisted of vertical walls of planks that varied in height from 4 to 6 feet (1.2–1.8 m). The bow, in contrast, was canted, or angled, like that of a modern barge to allow the boat to float more easily through the water. French traveler Victor Collot sketched one such flatboat that he encountered on the Ohio River in 1796 (Figure 2.1). A sketch of an early nineteenth-century ark also shows an angled bow (Figure 2.2).

Flatboats had a rectangular shape that gave them the appearance of floating shoe boxes. Pre–Civil War flatboats varied in length from 30 to 100 feet (9.1–30.5 m) although the majority appear to have measured between 40 and 60 feet (12.2–18.3 m) long. Width varied between 12 and 20 feet (3.7–6.1 m) depending on the length of the boat. Most pre–Civil War flatboats had width-to-length ratios of 1:2.5 or 1:3. Using these ratios, a 12-foot-wide (3.7 m) flatboat would have measured between 30 and 36 feet (9.1–11.0 m) long. Flatboats increased in size after the Civil War as their function shifted away from carrying travelers to transporting freight just as modern-day barges

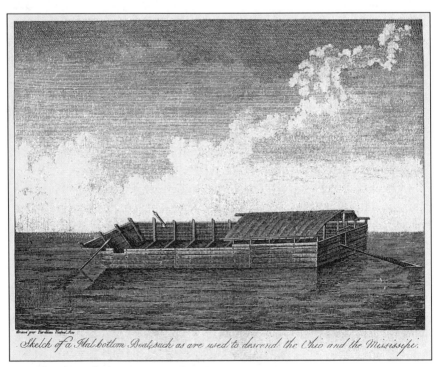

2.1. Ohio River flatboat, 1796. *Collot 1826.*

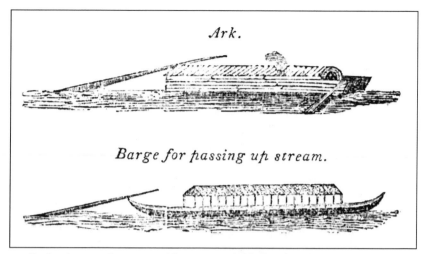

Ark.

Barge for passing up stream.

2.2. Early nineteenth-century Ohio River ark (flatboat) and barge. *Dunbar 1915.*

or cargo ships do. Lengths of 100 to 125 feet (30.5–38.1 m) became the rule rather than the exception, while widths varied from 18 to 25 feet (5.5–7.6 m). The typical width-to-length ratio appears to have increased to between 1:5 and 1:6. In other words, post–Civil War flatboats appear to have been considerably longer but not much wider than their late eighteenth- and early nineteenth-century predecessors.[22]

The superstructures of flatboats varied considerably, depending on the purpose of the boat and the skills of the boatbuilder. Emigrant, or "family," flatboats often contained a single structure in the center, with the stern and bow sections of the boat left open (Figure 2.3). A wooden flatboat model belonging to SIUC's University Museum that was built by artisans associated with the 1930s Works Progress Administration (WPA) gives a good idea of what this type of boat looked like (Figures 2.4–2.6). The boat is so correct in detail (except for the orientation of the floor planks, which run lengthwise rather than side-to-side) that it is possible that the model makers interviewed southern Illinois residents who had actually seen or built flatboats to learn what the boats looked like.

Livestock and cargo belonging to the family were carried in the open area of the boat, while the family slept and ate in the cabin (Figure 2.3). In other flatboats the cabin was near the stern (Figure 2.1). Rather than a cabin, the enclosed portion of the boat sketched by Collot was covered by an arched plank roof supported by stanchions, leaving a gap between the roof and the top strake of planks on the side of the boat. This rudimentary

2.3. Nineteenth-century "emigrant," or "family," flatboat. *Bryant 1872.*

2.4. Wooden flatboat model built by 1930s Works Progress Administration (WPA) artisans and now owned by SIUC's University Museum. The angled bow is similar to those on modern barges.

2.5. Stern, or back, view of the 1930s WPA flatboat model showing the boxlike shape of the flatboat hull. The side sweep attached to the cabin roof would have been used to help steer the boat.

2.6. Back, or stern, view of 1930s WPA model showing the cabin window and entrance as well as the ladder used to reach the cabin roof.

shelter provided a place for the crew to escape the weather, to sleep, and to cook their meals. Flatboats constructed primarily as cargo vessels, particularly those of the mid to late nineteenth century, often were completely roofed over, with no open deck space (Figure 2.7). Roof hatches allowed the crews to enter the cabin and cargo areas of the boat (Figure 2.8). Cabins on such flatboats could sometimes be quite elaborate, with bunks, fireplaces, tables, chairs, and other furnishings provided for the comfort of the travelers and crew.[23] French artist and naturalist Charles Lesueur sketched the interior of one such cabin as part of his 1828 journey down the Ohio River.[24] Lesueuer's sketches of his flatboat (Figures 2.9 and 2.10) reveal that the cabin contained a large brick fireplace, roof hatches that provided access to and egress from the cabin, and no furniture. Instead, the tops of barrels and crates were used as makeshift tables. Shelves and hooks along the cabin walls were used to store cups, buckets, bottles, and a coffee grinder (see Figure 2.10). The large brick fireplace contained a large pot or kettle set on top of a roaring fire. An irregular solid-colored area beneath the fire that extended from the front of the fireplace may represent a layer of sand laid down to protect the wooden floor. It is not surprising, given the size of the fire shown in Lesueur's sketch, that the brick lining of the fireplace failed to protect the wooden walls of the cabin from charring. To correct this problem, Lesueur and his companions reinforced the back of the fireplace with limestone slabs, which they obtained by dismantling a prehistoric Native American stone-lined grave they discovered at Cave in Rock, Illinois.[25]

2.7. Mid- to late nineteenth-century flatboat. *Ambler 1932.*

2.8. Traveler's Insurance ad of about the 1950s showing a man and a boy on top of a flatboat that has a roof hatch leading into the cabin. *Personal collection, Mark Wagner.*

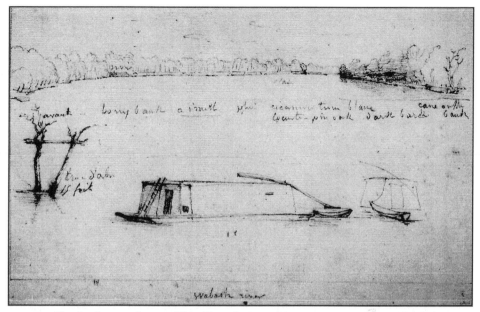

2.9. Charles Lesueur's 1826 Ohio River flatboat. *Hamy 1968.*

2.10. Interior of Charles Lesueur's 1826 Ohio River flatboat. *Hamy 1968:5.*

Flatboats were dependent on the river current as their primary source of power. Many of them also contained a secondary source of power in the form of a sail carried on a mast set on the cabin roof.[26] Lacking a rudder, flatboats were instead steered with long oars, or sweeps, at the stern and sides of the vessels. The number of oars varied between three and six depending on the size of the vessel. Smaller flatboats typically carried only three oars, consisting of a steering oar at the stern and two sweep oars on the sides (see Figures 2.1–2.3). During the late nineteenth century, steering oars reportedly measured 65 to 70 feet long, while the side sweeps were almost 40 feet long. Larger flatboats often contained two sweep oars on each side of the boat, which in combination with the steering oar gave them a total of five oars. Finally, some flatboats contained yet another oar, known as a "gouger," at the bow. It was used to throw the boat in another direction in a hurry when a hazard such as a snag, tree, or stump was spotted in front of the boat.[27]

How Do You Build a Flatboat?

Flatboats were constructed both in commercial shipyards and by settlers and merchants at various places along the Ohio and Mississippi Rivers. As early as 1788, Pittsburgh newspapers carried ads for flatboats built in commercial shipyards. Zadok Cramer, the author of an early nineteenth-century Ohio River guide known as *The Navigator*, advised his readers that "there are large boat-yards" at Pittsburgh, Wheeling, Brownsville, and other locations on the upper Ohio River where west-bound emigrants could purchase boats.[28]

There are a handful of firsthand accounts of the building techniques used in flatboat construction between 1830 and 1890 in Ohio, Indiana, and Illinois.[29] Although varying in detail, all of these histories agree on a basic set of construction methods. All, however, were written from memory long after the flatboat era had passed, and it is clear that some of the writers either forgot or simply left out some construction steps and techniques.

The initial step involved the creation of the chine-girders, or gunwales, that formed the two long sides of the flatboat. A pre–Civil War (1838–1846) Indiana flatboat builder named John Gilkeson noted that gunwales 13 inches (33 cm) thick by about 40 inches (1.0 m) wide were hewn from a log solely by using a chopping ax and a maul.[30] The southern Illinois flatboat merchant Daniel Harmon Brush similarly noted that for three flatboats he built in 1847 the "gunwales were hewn out of a large yellow poplar tree to a thickness of 8 inches and three feet, or as wide as the tree would square."[31] Later flatboat builders, such as Cliff Frank of Indiana, also used saws to help cut the log in two once the tree had been felled. Frank noted that for a flatboat he helped build in 1866, a large poplar tree up to a "hundred feet long . . . [and] six feet in diameter [was selected and] ripped . . . into two gunwales."[32] Ohio resident Captain Miles Stacy used both a broadax and a saw to cut out the gunwales on flatboats he built between 1849 and 1869. Stacy noted, "I'd get one large, straight yellow poplar tree about eighty or ninety feet long. I'd fell it . . . and hew it on both sides with a broad-ax to 18 inches thick. Then I'd shove it on to skids, line it through the centre and rip it in two with a whipsaw. This made each gunnel 9 inches thick and as wide as the tree would make them."[33]

Oxen and chains were used to drag the two gunwales to a local boatyard or work area near a stream bank where the real construction of the flatboat then began.[34] Gilkeson first cut a "slope" in the bottom of each several-foot-wide gunwale starting about 8 feet (2.4 m) from the bow end. The depth of the cut steadily increased toward the bow, at which point the gunwale was only 1 foot (30.5 cm) thick.[35] Colonel William Cockrum also noted that the gunwales of Indiana flatboats were "sloped from six to eight feet . . . so that [the boat] would run much faster in the water."[36] The other boatbuilding accounts do not mention this construction stage, and it is unclear how widespread this practice of sloping the bow section of the gunwale actually was.

The first step for the other boatbuilders involved cutting a rabbet, or ledge, into the inboard side of the bottom of each gunwale for their entire length. The depth of the rabbet was the same as the thickness of the floor planks, the opposing ends of which would rest on the rabbets. Brush cut a "rabbet 2 inches deep by six inches wide . . . on the bottom of each gunwale" to hold the ends of "2-inch poplar planks 20 feet long."[37] Frank stated that he cut 3-inch-deep (7.6 cm) rabbets on his 1866 flatboat but did not specify the width. Gilkeson cut much wider rabbets (10 inches [25 cm] wide, 2 inches [5 cm] deep) out of the gunwales on the flatboats he built between 1838 and 1846.[38]

Gilkeson next cut a series of evenly spaced tenons down the inboard sides of each of the gunwales to hold the mortise ends of the "cross-ties" that would eventually connect the two gunwales. He also cut a series of evenly spaced mortises into the tops of the two gunwales to hold the stanchions to which the side planks of the boat would eventually be pegged. The other boatbuilders do not mention this stage, although all of them had to at least have cut mortises into the girders at this point to hold the tenon ends of the cross-ties or they could not have laid the floor of the flatboat.

Log girders called "bow pieces" and "stern pieces" were then attached to the two ends of the gunwales using mortise-and-tenon joints, completing the rectangular framework of the hull bottom. Mortises also were cut into the inboard sides of the bow and stern pieces. The next step involved laying a series of evenly spaced cross-ties, or "cross-timbers," between the two gunwales. The cross-ties, or cross-timbers, on some boats were roughly shaped, being hewn on two sides only, and measuring about 8 inches (20.3 cm) thick.[39] The cross-ties had tenon ends that were inserted into the prepared mortises on the inboard sides of the two gunwales. A hole was then drilled through the tenon into the gunwale, and the tenon was pegged in place by driving a treenail into the hole. Gilkeson spaced his cross-ties 6 feet (1.8 m) apart,[40] meaning that a 60-foot-long (18.3 m) flatboat built to his specifications would have eight cross-ties to fill the area between the bow and stern girders. Stacy used a 7-foot (2.1 m) interval between cross-ties,[41] meaning that he could have built a 70-foot-long (21.3 m) boat using the same number of cross-ties (eight) as Gilkeson would have used in building a 60-foot-long boat. Cockrum of Indiana recalled an even wider interval, noting that "sills or girders were framed into the gunwales every eight or ten feet and securely fastened there by strong pins."[42]

The next step involved laying a series of small-diameter girders variously called "stringers," "streamers," or "sleepers" down the long axis of the boat. These stringers had tenon ends that were inserted into mortises in the stern and bow girders. Their ends were then pinned in place using treenails. Holes also were drilled though the stringers where they intersected the cross-pieces, and treenails were used to hold these two different types of members together. The number of stringers apparently varied according to the preferences or local building traditions followed by the different boatbuilders. Cockrum recalled a spacing of 1.5 feet (45.7 cm) between the stringers, meaning that an 18-foot-wide (5.49 m) boat would have had ten stringers.[43] Both Stacey and Gilkeson, in contrast, spaced their stringers at 2-foot (61 cm) intervals so that they would have used only seven stringers in constructing a boat of the same width.[44] Brush, who noted that he used only five stringers in building a 20-foot-wide (6.1 m) boat, must have used a 3.5-foot (1 m) interval.[45] Gilkeson was the only boatbuilder to supply information about the appearance of the stringers. He noted that they were "about 3 inches thick of divers widths as that was of no consequence. Some times they were sawed and joined on the [cross] girders and sometimes [they] were made by splitting and hewing small hickory trees, in some instances the entire length of the boat."[46]

The cross-ties and stringers provided a framework for the laying of the plank floor. The planks were laid transversely across the boat, with their ends resting on the rabbets on the inboard sides of the gunwales. The planks had the same thickness as the depth of the rabbet cut, creating a smooth bottom for the boat because the floor planks were flush with the gunwales. The size and thickness of the floor planks varied between different boatbuilders and by the width of the boat being constructed. Stacey and Cockburn used planks that measured 1.5 inches (3.8 cm) thick, while Brush and Gilkeson employed 2-inch-thick (5.1 cm) planks. Brush used poplar for the floor planks,[47] while the type of wood used by the other boat makers is unknown. The floor planks were pegged to both the gunwales and the streamers. Frank recalled that on the boat he helped build, the ends of the floor planks were first spiked to the gunwales so that they would not move while being drilled. Then "with a two-inch augur, we bored holes and put two-inch wooden pins in each end of the board. The pins fit so that they were hard to drive in. Soon as they got wet nothing could pull them out."[48] Brush noted that the floor planks on his boat were "well pinned on [to the gunwales] with one-inch tough wood pins, and also pinned to each of the five stringers . . . and well secured at each end, front and rear [girders], to make strong support for the bottom planks."[49] Gilkeson, who clearly appears to have been the most exacting of the flatboat builders, noted that "two auger holes [were drilled through the ends of each plank] with [one] inch [diameter] augers . . . some 3 or 4 inches [deep] into the gunwales. Then tight fitting wooden pins of oak . . . were made as tight as they dare be made not to split the plank." Gilkeson also noted that "two holes [also were] bored [into each plank,] one every streamer. If there were five in the boat it required 14 pins in each plank, two in each streamer . . . in every plank the whole length of the bottom of the boat."[50]

Once the planks had been laid, the bottom of the boat was caulked to seal the spaces between the boards and make the boat watertight.[51] Cockrum noted that the "old Indiana flatboat builders used hemp for calking, driving it into the edges of the planks with a calking chisel made for the purpose."[52] The first step of caulking (or calking) a large vessel such as a flatboat involved laying oakum (a stringy, loose hemp fiber created by taking apart old ropes) that had been twisted into a strand into the open seam. A wooden caulking mallet was then used in combination with a "set iron" to drive the oakum into the seam. The oakum was then further compressed into the seam and sunk below the surface through use of a "making iron," which had a blunt or creased bit edge. The seam was then filled with pitch.[53] The seams of smaller vessels could be sealed in a one-step process using a single set iron. This involved twisting the "oakum into a loose cord of a size that will fit nicely into the seam," dipping it piece by piece into the pitch until it was saturated, then driving "it into the openings hard and firm with sharp . . . blows of [the caulking] chisel and mallet."[54]

Gilkeson followed the above procedure almost exactly in caulking the flatboats he built prior to the Civil War. He noted that on flatboats,

> every seam or joint betwixt two seams had to be calked. The calking consiste[d] of twisted cords of well broken hemp or flax ab[o]ut ¼ of an inch thick, and driven into the seams with an iron . . . calking chisel . . . [the blade edge of which was] about 1/16th of an inch and some 3 inches wid[e]. The edge [of the chisel] was fruted or guttered so as to take a better hold of the cord than if only a square. Of course, a mallet was used to drive the chisel. . . . After carefully calking all the cross seams [on the bottom of the boat], the side seams were particularly calked and sometimes pitched the pitch being made of rosin and lard and while still hot poured in small streams into all of the seams.[55]

Gilkeson's description of the caulking iron as having a "guttered" edge indicates he used a making iron, the edge of which is grooved down the center to compress the oakum into the seam and allow room for the insertion of the pitch.[56]

Up to this point, the various flatboats had been constructed in an upside-down manner similar to flat-bottomed building methods still followed in some parts of the world today.[57] That is, the gunwales had been set up with their upper edges facing downward so that the cross-ties, stringers, and floor planks could be pegged to the bottom of the boat. The next step in the procedure involved flipping the flatboat over so that the construction of the sides and the cabin could begin. Some of the flatboat builders clearly anticipated this stage by setting the gunwales on skids when they first began work on the boat. Cockrum recalled that the gunwales were set on a series of round logs on a slope leading down to the water. When it was time to launch the boat the builders set the logs rolling by inserting hand spikes into auger holes in the logs and turning them. As the logs began rolling the motion carried the boat down the slope and into the water.[58] Captain Miles Stacey followed a slightly different method. He apparently built his boat on skids that hung out over the top of the bank. One gunwale of the boat rested on the end of the skids that rested on land, while the other gunwale lay on the opposite end of the skids that extended out over the water. Then after "the skids were knocked out [the boat] slid into the water, bottom up."[59] Cliff Frank's crew followed yet another method. They apparently set skids between the boat and the water that extended out into the water. They then "put soft soap on the skids [and moved the boat onto the skids in some manner] and let her loose. The boat went into the deep water but not deep enough there to turn it over, the bottom side being up."[60]

At this point the boats described by Cockrum, Stacey, and Frank were upside down in the water. The boats now had to be flipped over and pulled back to shore. Cliff Frank's crew accomplished this by floating the boat downriver to a "deep place close to shore where there were big rocks and little rocks." They then nailed a board to the outside of one side of the hull and began stacking rocks against it. Eventually the weight of the rocks forced that side of the boat under water and "in going down it gave [the boat] enough momentum to turn it over." The crew also bored holes in the floor planks to break the suction between the water and the bottom of the boat. Once the hull had righted itself, they "drove pins in the holes in the bottom and bailed out what little water was left, and then towed the boat back up to [shore] . . . where we put the top on."[61] Captain Miles Stacey used a virtually identical method, noting that once the boat was in the water "we now placed [on it] three or four wagon loads of stone (three or four boards were [first] pinned on one side). Then we floated the boat into deep water, placed it across the stream and began quickly throwing the stones onto the downstream side, until weight and the current together caused the boat to turn over."[62]

William Cockrum and John Gilkeson described a different method involving ropes to flip their flatboats. Cockrum noted that similar to the first part of the method employed by Stacey and Frank, a "large amount of mud and dirt was piled on one edge of the [upside-down] bottom." But then, rather than letting gravity and momentum flip the boat, "a check line was fastened" to the opposite side of the boat. This line "was carried over a large limb or fork of a tree and two or three yoke of oxen hitched to it. When everything was ready, the boat turned right side up."[63] Gilkeson employed an even more refined method, sliding his upside-down boats from the shore into the water and flipping them over as part of a single procedure. Gilkeson built his flatboats on skids that extended partially over the water. When it came time to lower a boat into the water it was "prised by lever power until nearly on a balance. The gunwale [that extended] out over the water being secured to bank in such a way as to let it go down into the water but not any farther from the bank. [After the boat was] nearly on a balance it was not a hard matter to tip it up and turn it over."[64] Gilkeson does not explain how the boat was secured to shore or how the force needed to flip it over was generated, although he may have used an oxen-pulled rope draped over a tree limb, like the method described by Cockrum. After the boat was righted, it was bailed out with a wooden grain shovel and pulled back up onto shore.

Once the boats had been towed back to shore, the construction of their superstructure began. The first step involved cutting mortise holes in the tops of the gunwales to hold the vertical stanchions (also called studs or studding) to which the side planking of the boat was to be pegged. Daniel Harmon Brush noted that "studs were inserted into the upper edges of the gunwales and 2-inch [thick] plank [was pegged to the studs] to the height of say three feet above the tops of the gunwales."[65] Miles Stacey similarly noted that into the gunwales "we fitted our studding, which was five feet long. . . . Onto this we spiked or pinned 2-inch planks, 18 inches wide for the first course around the boat and [after that] 1½ inch plank as wide as we could get we placed above this."[66] As noted above, the side planking on the boats built by Brush and Stacey extended 3 to 5 feet above the top of the gunwale. The boat built by Cliff Frank's crew in 1866, however, apparently had even higher sides. He noted, "[We] put stanchions all around. That made it eight feet from the floor to the roof. Then the siding was spiked on to the stanchions. Then two rows of stanchions ran the full length of the boat in the middle, far enough apart for two barrels to be rolled lengthwise between them and two feet higher than the outside stanchions."[67] John Gilkeson provided the most detailed information regarding the stanchions and side planking of pre–Civil War flatboats. He cut a series of mortises spaced 4 feet apart in the tops of the gunwales. Then "studding of sawed oak timber about 3½ feet long" with 4½- to 5-inch tenons were "made to fit the aforesaid mortises." Mortises for uprights also were cut in the tops of the stern and bow pieces. Then "all studding and post now being ready [they] were driven into the mortices and . . . secured by wedging. . . . [N]ext two inch [wide] planks were pinned fast to studding and posts same as the bottom [planks of the boat]."[68]

Until this stage all four flatboat builders—Brush, Frank, Gilkeson, and Stacey—and Cockrum, who knew a great deal about flatboat construction but may not have built one, described a series of construction events that generally agreed with each other. These included splitting the gunwales into chine-girders, constructing the bottom of the boat upside down, attaching a lattice-like framework of cross-girders and stringers covered by a plank floor, flipping the boat over, and then adding the stanchions and side planking. The cabins or enclosed areas of the boats built by these men, however, appear to have varied depending on what they intended to use the boat for. Brush appears to have built simple curved roof shelters similar to the ones illustrated by Victor Collot in 1796[69] (Figure 2.1). Captain Miles Stacy, in contrast, may have completely enclosed his boat. Stacey noted that the curved roof of his boat was supported by at least one row of stanchions set inside the hull that were "18 inches higher than the side studding. Thus making the top slightly rounding, sloping to each side." A cabin about 6 feet deep and as wide as the width of the boat was at the stern of the flatboat. This cabin contained a "stove or fireplace for cooking, a table hinged on the wall, and at either end a bed, made of boards placed on top of a bin of potatoes. A pair of stairs led from the cabin to hatch-hole in roof. There were no windows."[70] Stacey's description of this cabin, with the exception of the window, suggests that it was similar to one sketched by Charles Lesueur in 1828. The boat built by Cliff Frank's crewmates also had a curved roof, but it was supported by two rows of stanchions. He remembered that "linn lumber was nailed on top of those stanchions, green, and it curved it was so limber. They usually put three layers on so it wouldn't leak, and about a two-by-six was spiked on along the outside edge, straight up from the gunwales, to hold the roof down on the outside. Linn is porous and in a little while becomes also a solid roof." Frank's boat contained a cabin in the stern similar to that described by Stacey. The cabin housed a "board table" as well as two bunks on each side that could hold four men each.[71] The flatboats built by John Gilkeson were completely enclosed, like the boat illustrated in Figure 2.7. Their curved roofs rested on a ridge pole supported by a single row of stanchions whose bottoms were set in the center of the cross girders. The roofs themselves consisted of several layers of oak and poplar planks that in their finished form resembled "an old fashioned clapboard roof."[72]

The boats built by these men contained from three to six long oars attached to the sides, stern, and bow. The number of oars to some degree was dependent on vessel length, with longer boats having an additional set of side sweeps. Cliff Frank's 1866 boat, for example, which appears to have measured 100 feet long, had "six sweeps, two on a side and one on each end. The [side oars] are the ones to pull on—the end ones are to guide with."[73] Brush's 60-foot-long 1847 flatboats, however, had only three oars consisting of "a long steering oar and two side oars, with the craft manned by a pilot at the steering oar . . . and four stout men to shove the sweep or side oars."[74] Miles Stacey remembered that the 80- to 90-foot-long flatboats he sailed on between 1849 and 1869 had four oars. These consisted of "a steering oar 65 or 70 feet long, fastened to the stern of the boat and reaching up over one-third of the boat's length. . . . The oars on either sides were called 'sweeps.' These were 38–40 feet long and placed one-third of the way back from the bow. Two men manned each sweep. . . . In front was a shorter oar called a 'gouger,' and about 30 feet long, also used in steering."[75] John Gilkeson's 60- to 80-foot-long 1838–1846 flatboats apparently contained only three oars, although Carmony's reconstruction of one of these boats shows it as having four oars.[76] The steering oar generally measured about "60 feet long and upwards" depending on the length of the boat. The length of the side sweeps similarly depended on the width of the boat. On a "16 ft wide [boat] they were 32 feet long and for a wider boat [they were] longer." The steering oar and sweeps were each made from a "strait [*sic*] bodied tree about 12 to 14 inches in diameter." Holes were drilled through the handles of the oars so that they could be inserted over wooden pins fastened on the roof of the flatboat. The side sweeps rested on pins set in wooden blocks fastened to the top of the roof. Similar to Captain Stacey's description, they were "set about one third of the length from the bow." The steering oar, in contrast, was hung on a hickory pin set within the top of an upright girder or "steering post" whose base rested in the center of the stern piece. The steering post extended up from the stern girder to slightly above the top of the cabin roof.[77] Finally, Cockrum also reports that Indiana flatboats contained three oars consisting of two side sweeps and a steering oar.[78]

Other Flat-Bottomed Boats on the Ohio and Mississippi Rivers

Flatboats represented only one of several different types of flat-bottomed plank vessels on the inland rivers of the United States during the late eighteenth and the nineteenth centuries. Other plank vessels known to have been present on the Ohio and Mississippi Rivers during this time included skiffs, wharf boats, barges (Figure 2.2), peddler's boats, houseboats, ferryboats, and church boats. Wharf boats essentially functioned as floating warehouses at which steamboats could unload and pick up cargo regardless of the river level. Skiffs were flat-bottomed low-profile rectangular vessels that lacked plank sides. Also called lighters, these craft were used to carry merchandise, passengers, and wood between steamboats and the shore or between steamboats and wharf boats tied to the shore.[79] Many flatboat crews also used a "painter" or rope to attach to the vessel stern a skiff that they could use in emergencies (see Figure 2.9).

Historian Reuben Gold Thwaites photographed a number of flat-bottomed vessels, including houseboats, shanty boats, barges, merchant boats, church boats, skiffs, and barges, during an 1894 boat trip down the entire length of the Ohio River.[80] Thwaites's photographs of these boats, especially the larger ones such as houseboats and church boats, indicate that in many aspects they were strikingly similar to nineteenth-century flatboats.[81] Common characteristics included rectangular shape, canted bow sections, and enclosed cabins amidships or in the stern. The primary difference between these vessels and flatboats is that the former appear to have been shallow-draft vessels that lacked high plank sides. It is unclear from the photographs, however, whether any of these boats had log gunwales similar to those on a flatboat.

The similarity in appearance of many of these boats to flatboats suggests that they may have derived from and been part of the same Ohio River flat-bottomed boatbuilding tradition. It also appears that some of the larger vessels may have been abandoned flatboats converted to local use as the flatboat era drew to an end in the late nineteenth century. Particularly notable in this regard are the three large "junk boats" and a "church boat" photographed by Thwaites.[82] Thwaites's photographs show the roofs of the cabins as being completely covered with barrels and other cargo. Thwaites described the operators of these boats:

> merchant peddlers, who spend a day or so at some rustic landing, while scouring the neighborhood for oil-barrels and junk, which they load in great heaps upon the roofs of their cabins, giving . . . [in exchange] groceries, crockery, and notions—often bartering their wares for eggs and dairy products, to be disposed of to passing steamers.[83]

The junk boats lacked engines and apparently were still powered by oars or sweeps, although none are evident in the published photographs.

Thwaites noted in his diary, however, that he had rushed down to the river to photograph one "junk-boat just putting off into the stream" that was powered by "two rough-bearded, merry-eyed fellows at the sweeps."[84] His photograph of another junk boat tied to the shore shows that it had an upright stanchion behind the center of the bow that may have been intended to hold the "gouger" oar.[85] Finally, Thwaites's photograph of the *Owensboro Bethel*, a large church boat tied to the shore at Owensboro, Kentucky, shows that this vessel had an off-center mast on the port side of the boat forward of the cabin. Two "sheets," or support ropes, extended from the top of the tall mast to the two stern corners of the cabin roof. In addition, what may be the handle section and part of the body of a long curved steering oar at the stern of the boat are barely visible in the photograph.[86]

The flatboat tradition of the Ohio and Mississippi Rivers never really ended but continues today in the form of large rectangular metal flat-bottomed barges built in commercial shipyards. Now pushed by diesel-powered towboats rather than floating with the current and being steered or powered by men pulling on wooden sweeps, these modern-day barges loaded with coal or other industrial products are the direct descendants of the 200-year-old wooden flat-bottomed boatbuilding tradition of the inland waterways of the midcontinental United States.

3. Dashed to Pieces: Flatboat Wrecks on the Ohio and Mississippi Rivers

*T*raveling down the Ohio and Mississippi Rivers in box-shaped boats that could be only crudely steered was an extremely risky enterprise that resulted in hundreds, if not thousands, of wrecks over the approximately 130 years of the flatboat era (Figure 3.1). Flatboat wrecks often clustered in areas of the river that were dangerous for one reason or another. One such place was Flour Island in the lower Mississippi River that was "so called for the number of flour Boats wrecked upon it, t'is said as many as 15 in one year."[1]

Timothy Flint, writing in 1826, also gave the impression that numerous boat wrecks littered the banks and islands of the Mississippi River. Looking back on his experiences over the previous ten years, he noted, "I do not remember to have traversed this river in any considerable trip, without having heard of some fatal disaster to a boat, or having seen a dead body of some boatman. . . . The multitudes of carcasses of boats, lying at the points, or thrown up high and dry on the wreck-heaps, demonstrate most palpably, how many boats are lost on this wild . . . river."[2]

French traveler Victor Collot believed that flatboats sank in such great numbers because "these boats are constructed without nails, which renders them very dangerous for the Mississippi, in which great numbers perish by the damage which they receive from the least shock, either against rocks, or great trees with which this river is sometimes choked, as well as by the difficulty of steering."[3]

Flatboats, however, wrecked and sank for a number of reasons, both cultural and natural, rather than simply because they were built without iron nails. In the following section I examine some of the reasons in detail

3.1. Abandoned Ohio River raft (*foreground*) and flatboat (*background*) wrecks sketched by Charles Lesueur near Fort Massac in 1828. *Bonnemains 1984.*

to provide a background for the investigation of the possible factors behind the sinking of the *America* flatboat.

How to Wreck a Flatboat

Rotten Wood and Injured Planks

Early nineteenth-century river travelers who lacked the time or expertise to build their own flatboat could buy one from a number of shipyards on the upper Ohio River near Pittsburgh. Boatyards in downriver cities such as Cincinnati and Louisville constructed flatboats for sale as well. Ohio River guide Zadok Cramer noted that flatboats could be bought at a number of shipyards on the upper Ohio, with Brownsville, Pittsburgh, and Wheeling being the main points of embarkation.[4] He warned prospective buyers, however, to have flatboats carefully inspected by persons knowledgeable about boat construction before purchasing a boat "owing to the unpardonable carelessness and penuriousness of the boat builder, who will frequently slight his work or make it of injured [rotten] plank . . . putting the lives and properties of a great many persons to manifest hazard." Poor workmanship and the use of rotten wood in flatboat construction apparently were so wide-spread on the upper Ohio that Cramer believed this egregious misconduct could only be solved by the "appointment of a boat inspector at different places" along the upper Ohio River. As an example of the danger of the use of "injured plank" Cramer cited an 1807 court case where a flatboat pilot who had lost his boat by hitting a submerged rock had been sued by the boat owner for carelessness and the loss of the cargo. The pilot cleared himself by bringing into court a section of floor planking from the wreck that revealed the bottom of the boat had given way in the accident because it had been built from rotten wood.[5]

Pirate Attacks

Stories about pirates on the lower Ohio River during the late eighteenth and early nineteenth centuries are many.[6] Pirates were said to have attacked innumerable boats, murdering their crews and then taking the hijacked boats and their cargo downstream to the Mississippi River and New Orleans. Pirates who reportedly operated from Cave-in-Rock in the early 1800s include Samuel Mason and the notorious Harpe brothers.

Did any of these people really exist? Some of these "pirates," as it turns out, were fictional characters in the overblown tall tales about the American frontier that delighted early nineteenth-century American readers. Court cases and other documents, however, reveal that pirates indeed did exist along the Ohio and Mississippi Rivers, with the few detailed accounts of their activities being more than gruesome enough to make up for all the fictional tales of piracy along these two rivers.

• • •

The most credible accounts of piracy on the lower Ohio River are those involving Samuel Mason, an extremely violent Revolutionary War veteran who attacked, looted, and burned flatboats on the Ohio and Mississippi Rivers from at least 1782 to 1803.[7] Captured by the Spanish in 1803, Mason and one of his gang members turned on each other at a preliminary inquest held in New Madrid, Missouri, and offered testimony that revealed they had robbed and burned numerous boats on the Ohio and Mississippi Rivers for over 20 years. In addition to their testimony, the Spanish discovered grisly firsthand evidence of Mason's crimes when they found the scalps of 20 murdered travelers hidden among his possessions. This evidence was more than enough to convince the local authorities he was a pirate, and they dispatched him under guard to the Spanish seat of government in New Orleans. There the Spanish governor, who was in the process of transferring New Orleans to the United States as part of the Louisiana Purchase, declared he had no time to deal with Mason and ordered him sent back upriver under guard to the American governor of Mississippi Territory.

Shortly before they reached Mississippi Territory in March 1803, Mason and one of his gang members seized a gun and killed the Spanish officer who had been in charge of conveying them back up the river. Mason jumped over the side of the boat to make his escape, only to be struck in the head by a lead musket ball fired by one of the other guards. Despite this serious injury, Mason managed to escape into the woods, although in all likelihood he died a short time later from his wound.

Mason's escape threw both the American and the Spanish authorities into an uproar, and a sizable reward was offered for his recapture. A few days after his escape two of his own gang members, in what can only be described as profound stupidity, brought his severed head to American authorities to claim the reward. There they had the misfortune to run into a flatboat owner who they had robbed only a short time before and as a result received a reward different from the one they had anticipated.[8] The two men were quickly arrested and tried in federal court not for Mason's murder, which they may or may not have committed, but for the crime of piracy.[9] Both were found guilty and hung in Greeneville, Mississippi Territory, in 1804.

Mason's death and the breakup of his gang appear to have largely ended organized piracy along the Ohio and Mississippi Rivers. While it is clear that attacks on flatboats continued after this date, no one seems to have risen to take Mason's place as the leader of a widespread gang of pirates and dishonest merchants. Botanist Thomas Nuttall reported that prior to 1811 "there existed on the banks of the Mississippi, a very formidable gang of swindling robbers . . . about 80 in number . . . under the direction of two captains . . . usually stationed at the mouth of the Arkansa [*sic*], and at Stack Island."[10] Nuttall had no firsthand knowledge of these pirates, however, and this may be a garbled account of Mason's activities in the same two areas a decade earlier.

Other accounts of post-1803 banditry along the two rivers include an entry made by John James Audubon in his diary during an 1820 flatboat trip down the Mississippi River. According to Audubon, the flatboat captain pointed out a bend in the river near Wolf Island on the Mississippi, another reported hangout of pirates, where he had found the bodies of two "dead men shot through the head" on a previous voyage.[11]

Yet another instance involved James Ford, a dishonest ferry operator and tavern keeper suspected of numerous robberies and murders along the lower Ohio River in the 1820s and 1830s.[12] Ford placed an advertisement in an Illinois newspaper in 1832 seeking the return of a runaway slave who had "both ears cut off close to his head, which he lost for robbing a boat on the Ohio River."[13] If even half the stories about Ford are true, he most likely was concerned, more than anything else, about his runaway slave escaping to somewhere he could talk freely about Ford's criminal activities.

Perhaps the most famous account of a "late" pirate attack on a flatboat is that involving future U.S. president Abraham Lincoln (Figure 3.2). In 1828, while a young man, Lincoln and a friend built a flatboat and took it down the Mississippi River to New Orleans. While the boat was tied to the shore one night below Baton Rouge, Lincoln recalled, "they were attacked by seven negroes with intent to kill and rob them. . . . [We] were hurt some in the melee, but succeeded in driving the negroes from the boat."[14]

While Samuel Mason's death may have marked the end of large-scale piracy along the Ohio and Mississippi Rivers, it also marked the beginning of a piracy folklore tradition that has continued to the present day. Among the earliest of the fictional pirates was Colonel Pfluger, or "Plug." Colonel Plug first appeared in two identical stories published in two separate literary magazines by romantic novelist and historian Timothy Flint in 1830.[15] Operating from the mouth of the Cache River, a small southern Illinois stream that drains into the Ohio, Colonel Plug and his fellow pirate "Nine-Eyes" reportedly plundered an unknown number of Ohio River flatboats and

3.2. Still from a 1920s silent movie showing Abraham Lincoln on a flatboat trip down the Mississippi River. The movie is early enough that this may have been an actual flat-bottomed river craft of some kind, although the steering oar held by Lincoln is clearly a prop. *Personal collection, Mark Wagner.*

First National

A FLATBOAT ON THE MISSISSIPPI—"ABRAHAM LINCOLN"

Abraham Lincoln guiding a flat boat on the Mississippi. This was the customary method of sending produce to a market in the West of those days.

murdered their crews. Colonel Plug's favorite method of operation consisted of sneaking unobserved onto a flatboat "to dig out the caulking in the bottom, or bore a hole in the hull." When the boat began to sink, Plug and his gang would loot the boat under the guise of salvaging it. Plug finally met his end when he failed to get off one of the sinking boats in time. As he attempted to grab a floating liquor barrel, it rolled over and Plug "drank water instead of whiskey, which he would have preferred . . . [and] he found a watery grave."[16]

Flint's stories of Colonel Plug fall squarely within the "half-horse, half-alligator" literary tradition of nineteenth-century Ohio River romantic fiction that also produced the Davy Crockett tall tales and other larger-than-life stories.[17] They have been reprinted so many times over the years, however, that their origin has been forgotten and Colonel Plug has come to be regarded as a real person.[18] In contrast to Captain Samuel Mason, however, whose existence is confirmed by numerous contemporary documents, Colonel Plug exists only in the two stories first written by Timothy Flint in the 1830s. Flint, in addition to being a missionary and a travel writer, also was founder and editor of a short-lived literary magazine called the *Casket* that printed fictional stories and poems. It seems Flint set out to write a tall tale about Colonel Plug's fictional adventures similar to the exaggerated stories written about Mike Fink and Davy Crockett. He appears to have based Colonel Plug on the very real and deadly pirate Samuel Mason.[19]

Attacks by Native Americans

Flatboat travelers descending the Ohio River prior to 1800 also faced the very real danger of attack by Native Americans. As early as the late 1760s a cargo boat belonging to the British trader George Morgan was ambushed near the mouth of the Cumberland River and its crew killed.[20] In late 1789 a Major Forman and his uncle departed Pittsburgh in a "fleet" of two keelboats and one flatboat bound for New Orleans. They wintered in Louisville, where they also took on a load of tobacco. While in Louisville, an American "renegade" or "decoyer, who lived among the Indians and whose job it was to lure boats ashore for the purposes of murder and robbery" learned the names of Forman and other members of his party. This man proceeded downriver ahead of Forman and attempted to lure Forman's party into an ambush near the abandoned French military post of Fort Massac:

At some point below the mouth of the Tennessee River, this renegade saw the boat approaching, ran on the beech [*sic*], imploring on his bended knees, that Mr. [Ezekiel] Forman, calling him by his name, would come ashore and take him in, as he had just escaped from the Indians. [My uncle] Mr. Forman began to steer for his relief, when Captain Osmon, who was a little in the rear, hailed uncle, warning him to keep to the middle of the stream, as he saw Indians hiding behind trees along the bank where the wily decoyer was playing his treacherous part. Giving heed to this admonition, Uncle Forman kept clear of the dangerous shore. . . . But for the circumstance of Captain Osmon . . . discovering the exposed Indians behind the trees, the whole party might have been lured on shore and massacred.[21]

The danger of attack by Native Americans on the lower Ohio appears to have increased markedly following the 1791 defeat and near-total destruction by Indian forces of the American Army under General Arthur St. Clair in Ohio. In response, General "Mad Anthony" Wayne dispatched Major Thomas Doyle down the Ohio River in 1794 to establish an American fort on the site of the former Fort Massac. In April 1795, Doyle's troops investigated the massacre of a party of 17 American flatboat travelers by Potawatomi and Kickapoo warriors at the junction of the Ohio and Cumberland Rivers above Fort Massac.[22] The following year Native Americans attacked and killed eight U.S. citizens near Grand Tower on the Mississippi River.[23] Indian attacks on the lower Ohio River appear to have decreased during the late 1790s as the U.S. military presence in the lower Ohio and Mississippi River valleys became more pronounced. River travelers on the lower Ohio, however, remained wary of attacks by the Cherokee into the first decade of the nineteenth century, although the threat of such attacks already had passed by this time.[24]

Collisions with Other Boats

Flatboats wrecked as the result of collisions with not only other flatboats but also their mortal enemy, the steamboat (Figure 3.3). Swift currents or high winds could push flatboats into each other, smashing their oars, at a minimum. Christian Schultz described one such incident that occurred during an 1808 nighttime voyage on the Mississippi River when the swift current pushed his boat into a group of 14 docked flatboats:

We were by this time blown so close in with the shore that we expected every moment to be wrecked. . . . [Suddenly] we discovered . . . lights ahead, and shortly after[,] we heard some voices calling us to pull in for the shore. This we immediately began to do, but not without great risk to ourselves, as well as to a part of a fleet of fourteen Kentuckians . . . against whom we were driven with so much violence as to break four pair of their [oar] sweeps by [their] endeavoring to keep us from dashing their boats to piece[s].[25]

The more powerful steamboats first appeared on the Ohio River in 1811. Many flatboats ran dark at night despite being required by law to keep a light on deck to warn steamboat pilots of their presence. Mark Twain recalled that such collisions were common on the Mississippi River prior to the Civil War, with each party blaming the other for the accident:

[Steamboat] pilots bore a mortal hatred to these small craft, and it was returned with usury. The law required all such helpless traders to keep a light burning, but it was a law that was often broken. All of a sudden, on a murky night, a light would hop up, right under our bows, almost, and an agonized voice with the backwoods "whang," to it, would wail out:
   "Whar'n the ——you goin' to! Cain't you see nothin', you dash-dashed aig-suckin', sheep-stealin', one-eyed son of a stuffed monkey!"
   Then for an instant, as he whistled by, the red glare from our furnaces would reveal the scow and the form of the gesticulating orator, as if under a lightning flash, and in that instant our firemen and deck-hands would send and receive a tempest of missiles and profanity, one of our wheels would walk off with the crashing fragments of a steering-oar, and down the dead blackness would shut again. And that flatboatman would be sure to go to New Orleans and sue our boat, swearing stoutly that he had a light burning all the time, when in truth his gang had the lantern down below to sing and lie and drink and gamble by, and no watch on deck.[26]

Natural Hazards: Planters, Sawyers, and Sandbars

Natural hazards such as low water, ice floes, earthquakes, strong winds, rocks, sandbars, sunken trees, collapsing banks, storms, and tornadoes were far more dangerous to flatboat travelers along the Ohio River than attacks by pirates or Native Americans. Sunken trees attached to the river bottom represented one of the most common and frightening menaces to river

3.3. Late nineteenth-century lithograph showing a steamboat and flatboat passing each other near Cave-in-Rock in southern Illinois. One wonders if they weren't cursing and throwing things at each other, similar to Mark Twain's description. *Personal collection, Mark Wagner.*

travel, as indicated by their mention in numerous early nineteenth-century accounts. Some tree trunks sank to the bottom, where the roots became embedded. Known as "planters," these stationary tree trunks extended up, daggerlike, through the water. If the trunk extended above the water the planter could be spotted and avoided by the flatboat crew. In many cases, however, the top of the tree trunk lay slightly beneath the surface and was not spotted by the crew until the boat ran upon it and the planter broke through the bottom of the boat. Daniel Harmon Brush described just such an accident that occurred to one of his flatboats on the Mississippi River in 1834:

> We were floating nicely, as we thought, in the current. No break of even a ripple appeared in the water ahead, or anywhere else about our boat. Suddenly and without premonition the bow began to rise in the water, seemingly ascending upon some solid substance fixed and stationary in the bottom of the river bed. Soon, however, the boat commenced settling in front and we discovered the sharp end of the snag had pierced the bottom of our boat and projected up through it about two feet. She was stopped in her course and firmly held in position, the bow end being just

above the water, and the stern at top just about even with the water. . . .
There we were suspended on Christmas day on the point of a deep-water
Mississippi snag, evidently the top of a large tree, the roots of which had
become securely embedded in the river's bottom at a place where our
lead line was not long enough to sound.[27]

Collisions with a planter could be repaired by hoisting the damaged part
of the boat out of the water, replacing the injured planks, and recaulking
the seams if the damage was not too bad.[28] Some flatboat crews, however,
lacked the tools or expertise to make such repairs, while in other cases the
damage simply was too great. While descending the Ohio River in 1796 a
crew of U.S. surveyors led by commissioner Andrew Ellicott came upon
a "Kentucky boat, fast upon a log, and . . . found that it was deserted, and
suspected that the crew were on shore in distress." Upon searching they
found several emigrant families huddled together on the shore in the snow
without any food or shelter "who had left the boat two days before . . . when
they found their strength insufficient to get her off." Ellicott and his men
managed to get the boat off the planter in two hours and towed it to shore
"where we received the thanks of the unfortunate crew."[29]

Frontiersman Daniel Trabue had a much worse encounter with a planter
while traveling with a party of five flatboats carrying 200 to 300 emigrants,
their livestock, and other possessions down the Ohio River to Kentucky in
1785. As he described it,

> [All of a] sudden our boat stove against the End of a log that was under
> the water. The boat came to a sudden stop, and all the horses and people
> fell down. . . . I saw there was a plank bursted [sic] at my end and the water
> coming in very rapid. We were 40 to 50 feet from shore. . . . I hollowed
> [sic] out for the woman [sic] and children to go to the end and Jump out,
> and the men to [throw] out the things. My end began to sink very soon,
> and I and another man cut the ropes that tyed [sic] the horses, and as
> the boat sunk the horses swom [sic] out. I think from the moment the
> boat struck the log until it sunk was not longer than three Minuts [sic].[30]

Far more feared by river travelers than planters, however, were the
sunken trees called "sawyers." Although, like planters, the roots of sawyers
were fixed in the river bottom, the upper part of the tree rose and fell in a
cyclical fashion. This was due to a combination of the natural buoyancy of

the wood, which caused the top of the tree to rise as much as 10 feet above the surface of the river,[31] and the river current, which flowed over the tree and forced it back under water. Sawyers could not be spotted easily, and flatboat crews often were unaware they were in danger until the water began to roil and bubble in front of their boat and the top of the sawyer emerged from the river. Traveler John Bradbury provided a vivid description of the appearance of the sawyers that he encountered during an 1810 voyage down the Mississippi River:

> [Although] they do not remove from where they are placed, [sawyers] are constantly in motion: the whole tree is sometimes entirely submerged by the pressure of the stream, and carried to a greater depth by its momentum than the stream can maintain. On rising, its momentum in the other direction, causes many of its huge limbs to be lifted above the surface of the river. The period of this oscillatory motion is sometimes of several minutes duration. These . . . *sawyers* . . . are much more dangerous than the *planters*, as no care or caution can sufficiently guard against them. The steersman this instant sees all the surface of the river smooth and tranquil, and the next he is struck with horror at seeing just before him the *sawyer* raising his terrific arms, and so near that neither strength nor skill can save him from destruction. This is not figurative: many boats have been lost in this way, and most particularly those descending [the river].[32]

Late eighteenth-century French traveler Victor Collot believed that planters and sawyers formed such a great danger to flatboats because of the "difficulty of steering" the boats out of danger at a moment's notice using the large steering oar at the back of the boat:

> The great oar placed at the stern, with which the Americans govern the boat, is extremely dangerous, from the difficulty of making it change its direction with sufficient speed to avoid the great trees and trunks that frequently obstruct the passage, and on which without great precautions, the boats are driven by the stream.[33]

Rocky stretches of the Ohio and Mississippi Rivers, especially in areas where the channel narrowed, also represented very real hazards to flatboats, with their limited maneuverability. High winds and storms often could dash flatboats against rocks or the shore despite the best efforts of the crew. In January 1806, one Ohio River traveler encountered high winds near Cave-in-Rock that threatened to dash his boat against a rocky shoreline. As he noted in his journal, "Last night was a time of trial . . . about 3 in the morning, blustering wind drove us towards the [Kentucky shore], which was dangerous by reason of rocks, all hands were raised and [rowed] hard for the Indiana [Illinois] shore." Two days later this same traveler commented further on the danger posed by rocks in the Ohio River, noting that "the eastern side of [Hurricane Island] is reckoned extremely dangerous to pass, excepting in high water, for reason of rocks, snags, and shoals."[34]

Thomas Rodney encountered numerous rock ledges and shoals while descending the Ohio River in 1803. He found the river so rock-choked near present-day Grand Chain "that we found it difficult to git [sic] through among the rocks to the shore."[35] Daniel Harmon Brush also commented on the danger of rocks in the Big Muddy River, a tributary of the Mississippi River in southwestern Illinois. Brush, an experienced river traveler, noted that at the very start of his 1847 flatboat trip down that river on his way to New Orleans "we passed the . . . large stone in the middle of the [Big Muddy] stream on which numerous boats had been wrecked."[36]

Sudden drops in the river level could leave flatboats stranded on sandbars. Flatboats also could be driven onto sandbars and islands by high winds or swift currents. Zadok Cramer repeatedly warned Ohio River travelers of the danger posed by sandbars, particularly noting that there were "two ugly sandbars" near Hurricane Island.[37] Daniel Brush recounted several incidents of his pre–Civil War flatboats being stranded on sandbars, sometimes for months, by rapid drops in the river level.[38] While passing through the Grand Chain of Rocks midway between present-day Cairo and Metropolis, Illinois, 1807 traveler John Bedford saw "three flat boats on ground and narrowly escaped grounding ourselves—were saved only by sounding [the depth of the river]." Bedford also encountered a stranded flatboat on a sandbar in the Mississippi River above New Madrid, the master of whom informed Bedford "they been grounded twenty days."[39] The anonymous author of an 1806 account of a flatboat trip down the Ohio River had to weave his way between two large sandbars at the mouth of the Cache River that had claimed at least one boat. He described this passage as "narrow and somewhat difficult. . . . [T]he left hand bar appeared most dangerous and has the wreck of a boat lying on it."[40] Thomas Rodney, whose detailed description of the lower Ohio River indicates that it was literally choked with sandbars in 1803, grounded at least twice but was able to get his boat off. Other travelers were not so fortunate. Rodney reported that a shoal or shallow area at the confluence of the Wabash and Ohio Rivers contained "the wrecks of a great number of arks . . . and like to have run on one in the middle of the river [ourselves]."[41]

Ice represented one of the greatest dangers to Ohio River travelers who made the journey downriver from December to February. Zadok Cramer called the winter months, when ice was on the river, "above all other seasons . . . the most perilous for travelers."[42] Floating ice pushed by the current could crush boats or break them against the shore. Commissioner Andrew Ellicott found out exactly how dangerous ice on the Ohio River could be when he landed near the confluence of the Ohio and the Mississippi on December 18, 1796. Temperatures had been above freezing the day he landed but dropped sharply in the next few days. The water level of the Ohio River dropped as well, leaving Ellicott's boats stranded on the bank and "frozen . . . fast in the mud." Meanwhile, the Ohio and Mississippi became so choked with ice that "each appeared like a vast mass of ice and snow in motion." Ellicott and his men, who feared that a sudden rise in the Ohio could cause the ice to break up and crush their boats, "laboured hard . . . to free the boats from ice and loose their bottoms from the mud and sand, and every person was now engaged to save them." Suddenly, the ice began to break up, causing the water to rise about four feet. This broke one of the boats free from the frozen mud, enabling it to be pulled onshore. The moving ice also broke the other boat free from the frozen ground, pushing it about 80 yards downstream, where it became wedged in the ice but "received no material injury." Although they had saved their boats, Ellicott and his men remained trapped by ice for another seven weeks. During this time both rivers were covered with moving ice "in so great a mass, that the water was not to be seen. . . . The concussion of the ice . . . produced a constant rumbling noise, for many hours, similar to that of an earthquake."[43]

Daniel Brush also encountered dangerous ice when he descended the Mississippi River below St. Louis in January 1835 on his way to New Orleans. The ice "rasped and grated along the side of the boat . . . all night long with an ominous sound" as Brush's flatboat descended the Big Muddy River. Brush's pilot thought it too dangerous to leave the Big Muddy and "strike out among the floating ice" on the Mississippi, but Brush overruled him, believing the ice would only become worse if they waited. They quickly found themselves at "the mercy of the floating ice" that surrounded the boat and made "it impossible to move right or left. As the ice around us went, we went." The moving ice continued to push the boat downriver, causing Brush to worry that they would "be crushed against the bank, an island, or by great masses of ice." Not until they had been pushed past the confluence of the Ohio and Mississippi did the ice begin to break up, once again freeing the boat.[44]

Flatboats also could be damaged or destroyed by collapsing riverbanks, especially on the powerful Mississippi River. While descending the Mississippi River below the mouth of the Ohio River in 1815, William Richardson tied his flatboat to "a willow which is always to be preferred as the land where they grow is flat—no danger from its caving in which is often the case at a [high] bold shore . . . where large trees grow. Not infrequently several acres are seen falling in at once and it is this which makes the planters and the sawyers."[45] Zadok Cramer also warned Mississippi River navigators about the danger of collapsing banks:

[Never] land at a point, but always in the sinuosity (i.e., curve) or cove below it. . . . The instability of the banks . . . and the impetuosity of the current against their prominent parts (points) . . . [undermines] them unceasingly [and] causes them to tumble into the river, taking with them everything that may be above. And if, when the event happens boats should be moored there, they must necessarily be buried in the common ruin, which unfortunately sometimes has been the case.[46]

Flatboats also sank in heavy storms that swamped their interiors or dashed them onto the shore or rocks in the river. The French artist Charles Lesueur traveled down the Mississippi in 1829 in what seemed to be a never-ending storm. Lesueur recorded in his diary that one particularly bad squall sank a flotilla of 12 flatboats, 60 to 80 feet long by 15 feet wide, that had been traveling down the river together. The cargoes that went down with these boats included corn, flour, lumber, hides, deer antlers, wax, bacon, deer haunches, poultry, and live pigs.[47]

Timothy Flint also warned travelers of the dangers of Mississippi River storms, noting that "they are at least as dangerous as they are on the sea." He vividly described one such storm in 1818 in which at least two boats with which his keelboat was traveling sank, one with its entire crew:

No person, who is unacquainted with the Mississippi, can have an adequate idea of the roughness and the agitation occasioned by a tempest, . . . The waves came in on the running-boards . . . of the boat, at times two feet deep. . . . Two very large boats, that came in company with us from the mouth of the Ohio, that had been lashed together before the storm, unlashed as the storm commenced. The one went on a sawyer, and was dashed to pieces. She had been loaded with four or five hundred barrels of flour, porter, and whiskey, and the barrels were floating by us in all directions. The hands left the other, that was loaded in the same way, and she floated by us, sunk to the roof. We made every effort to run her on shore in vain. Nor did we ever ascertain what became of the hands of the first boat. They probably all perished. For the water was over the banks from ten to twenty feet, and the width of this overflow was probably forty miles.[48]

On the basis of these and other accounts, the shores of the Ohio and Mississippi appear to have been literally covered with wrecked and abandoned flatboats during the nineteenth century, and it is surprising that many more flatboat wrecks have not been found. Wrecked flatboats, however, would have represented a ready source of sawn lumber for local settlers, who may have dismantled many of these wrecks as soon as they found them. Still others were most likely destroyed when the almost annual flooding of the Ohio and Mississippi swept their superstructures away. But as the discovery of the *America* wreck indicated, the remains of some of these wrecks may still exist at various locations along the Ohio River and smaller rivers, like the Cumberland, the Tennessee, and the Wabash, that feed into the Ohio. These wrecks, if they indeed are still out there, almost certainly consist only of the fragmentary remains of the gunwales and floor planks and, as such, may be hard to identify and separate from all the other debris that litters the shores of these rivers.

4. Stuck in the Mud: Documenting the *America*

$\mathcal{A}$ resident of southern Illinois, John Schwegman, discovered the *America* wreck in September 2000 while collecting mussels along the Ohio River during a period of extremely low water. Although the boat must have been periodically exposed on the banks of the Ohio for almost 200 years, John apparently was the first person in a long time to recognize it for what it was. He asked permission of an adjacent landowner to investigate the wreck, and assisted by several volunteers, he excavated the interior of the wreck and photographed the uncovered floor planks and other structural elements. A map of the wreck, however, was not completed.[1]

The wreck, which consisted of the stern and parts of the two gunwales, appeared to be 45 feet long by 12 feet wide. The bow, which had been pointed upstream, was missing. Interior features included the aft sections of two bow-to-stern stringers, parts of three cross-ties, floor planks, and a cluster of bricks approximately 4 feet in diameter. The floor planks were relatively intact at the stern but progressively more fragmentary toward the forward section of the boat, eventually disappearing altogether. The base of an upright stanchion to which the side planks of the hull would have been attached still rested in a mortise hole in the top of the stern girder. A "beam" also extended diagonally between the aft section of the starboard gunwale and the stern girder. One end of this beam rested on the interior ledge or rabbet of the gunwale, while the other end rested on the stern girder. Schwegman interpreted this wooden member as possibly having "supported the steering mechanism or may have been a brace."[2]

The bricks, which may have represented the remains of a platform for a stove, were scattered around and on top of the second cross-tie, approximately 18 to 22 feet north of the stern along the port gunwale. The excavators removed the bricks from the boat without mapping them and placed them in a pile outside and west of this gunwale before exposing the interior of the boat. Artifacts found within the wreck included an iron caulking chisel, three pewter spoons, a broken redware bowl, a pewter button, a broken iron tube, two bone-plated utensil handles, nails, and rusted iron.[3]

Upon the completion of their excavations, Schwegman and the other volunteers removed the diagonal wooden member that extended from the aft starboard gunwale to the stern girder so that it would not wash away. They also cut off a 2.6-foot-long section of the forward part of the broken port gunwale for wood identification purposes. The boat interior apparently was not backfilled or covered.

By examining the recovered artifacts, John Schwegman correctly interpreted the wreck as dating to the latter part of the eighteenth or the early part of the nineteenth century. He believed that the types of artifacts recovered indicated that the boat "carried passengers rather than freight" and possibly even livestock. He also suggested that although the reason the boat sank was unclear, the fact that its "wooden planks . . . and artifacts . . . (were not) salvaged . . . could point to foul play."[4] He identified the likely culprit as being Colonel Plug, the legendary river pirate who reportedly had his headquarters at the mouth of the Cache River only a few miles below the wreck site.[5] He also suggested that the orientation of the wreck, with the bow pointing upstream, as well as the burned exterior of the redware bowl, indicated that the boat may have been on fire and sunk as a result of a pirate attack.

The investigation of the *America* by volunteers in 2000 was not without controversy and should serve as a cautionary warning to others who find the remains of shipwrecks along the Ohio River shoreline. Despite what people may think, shorelines such as those bordering major rivers and oceans are often public rather than private property. Nineteenth-century shipwrecks, such as the *America,* that are historic properties more than fifty years old, are protected by state and federal law if they are on public land. Although the owner of the land adjoining the Ohio River where the *America* rests believed he could give permission to people to excavate the wreck, property rights in Illinois are interpreted by the state as ending at the water's edge rather than extending into the river. As such, the Illinois Historic Preservation Agency believed that the state of Illinois—not the owner of the adjacent land—owned the wreck, which is exposed only at extremely low river levels. This claim was contested by the Kentucky State Historic Preservation Office, which claimed that despite the wreck being on the Illinois shoreline, it actually belonged to the state of Kentucky. This claim was based on evidence of the boundaries of Kentucky during the late 1700s that show Kentucky owning all of the Ohio River at this location. In addition, the U.S. Army Corps of Engineers, which controls all waterways in the United States, asserted its jurisdiction over the wreck and allowed no excavations at the site without a permit from that agency.

Professional archaeologists, as well as everyday citizens, are subject to these regulations. As such, we at Southern Illinois University Carbondale (SIUC) had to obtain the necessary permits and permissions from all three of the above-mentioned agencies before we could conduct any work at the wreck site. We first obtained a permit and funding from the Illinois Historic Preservation Agency for the archaeological documentation of the wreck. The state of Kentucky, although it refused to give up its claim to the wreck, allowed our investigations to go forward, as they were being conducted by professional archaeologists. Finally, we had to obtain a nationwide permit from the Louisville District Corps of Engineers that allowed us to disturb the river shoreline (i.e., remove the fill from the wreck and map it) in a very limited fashion.

We initially visited the site of the *America* wreck in early August 2001. At that time the wreck was submerged, with only a portion of the gunwale extending out of the water (Figure 4.1). It was not until August 7, 2002, when the Ohio River dropped to 11 feet on the Cairo gauge, that the wreck was completely exposed and we could begin work (Figure 4.2). Because of uncertainty about how long the river would remain at this level, as well as the fact that the fill within the boat interior already had been severely disturbed, the documentation of the architecture of the wreck became our primary goal. This work followed the guidelines for recording historic ships presented in Anderson and Krisman in conducting this work.[6]

The beach surrounding the wreck consisted of an almost continuous heavy scatter of broken glass, ceramic, metal, plastic, and other objects dating from the early nineteenth to the late twentieth century. Artifacts included broken bottles, dishes, crocks, toys, cut nails, spikes, bars, hooks, musket balls, cans, buckets, metal boat parts, animal bones, plastic milk jugs and cartons, and many other objects. The Ohio has been a major transportation route since the beginning of the nineteenth century, and much of this debris undoubtedly represents trash lost or thrown from passing boats. Some of the debris also may be associated with now-vanished nineteenth- and twentieth-century structures along the riverbank that have eroded into the river. Still other items, most notably iron crowfoot hooks,

4.1. Unveiled parts of the normally submerged *America* flatboat in the Ohio River. What appears to be a log in the lower left-hand corner of this photograph is actually the edge of the starboard (right) gunwale of the wreck that was exposed as the river level began to drop in 2002. The barges in the background are direct descendants of flatboats.

4.2. Silted flatboat wreck a day or so after water receded from it in 2002. The soil surrounding the wreck is darker and wetter than the dryer upper bank. Author Mark Wagner (*third from left, with white baseball cap*) stands next to the left gunwale of the boat.

are the remains of "clamming" activities associated with a large mussel bed only a short distance from and within sight of the wreck. Because of the extent of debris and the range of its origins, we considered only those nineteenth-century artifacts recovered from within the wreck or within an approximately 5-meter radius to be associated with it.

The boat interior had completely refilled with river-deposited sand, muck, and driftwood in the two years following the September 2000 investigations (Figure 4.3). The northern, or bow, end of the boat contained several large logs as well as a number of smaller tree limbs and various other pieces of driftwood. The current had carried these logs into the boat, ramming them under the floor planks and lifting and breaking loose many planks in the forward section of the wreck. The northernmost of the two east-west cross-stringers had been lifted out of place and thrown at a diagonal across the stern section of the boat. And the upright stanchion fragment in the stern girder had washed away.

We removed the driftwood without mapping it, leaving the displaced boat planks and stringers in place. We then removed the fill within the boat through a combination of shoveling and troweling (Figures 4.4 and 4.5).

4.3. Close-up of the silt-covered wreck. The river has deposited logs and other driftwood within the hull.

4.4. Volunteer Bob Swenson (*far right*) and SIUC students begin removing the fill covering the wreck. All the soil was eventually screened to recover artifacts, most of which represented fill that had washed in after the wreck.

4.5. Bryan Carlo removing the last of the dirt fill to expose the wooden floor planks of the wreck and the longitudinal stringers to which they had once been pegged.

Screening of the mucky fill through quarter-inch mesh revealed that it consisted almost entirely of washed-in soils. Objects within this fill included river gravel, mussels, fish bones, late nineteenth- and twentieth-century bottle glass, cut nails, unidentifiable iron, and iron crowfoot mussel-fishing hooks identical to those materials on the beach surrounding the boat. Some of these items were pressed against the floor planks, indicating that the boat contained little in the way of intact early nineteenth-century materials. Screening of the boat fill subsequently was restricted to areas that John Schwegman indicated possibly still contained some undisturbed deposits. This focus resulted in the recovery of several redware vessel fragments, two metal clothing buttons, and an olive-green bottle neck.

Gunwales and Floorboards: Mapping the America Wreck

Using the metric system, we mapped the remains of the *America* by laying a boxlike grid of mapping points around and over the boat (Figures 4.6 and 4.7). We aligned the direction north with the long axis of the boat (which actually was slightly east of true north as shown on a compass), because it made mapping the wreck easier. Because of the lack of any permanent landmarks in the area of the boat, we tied our grid into a stake 12 meters southwest of the boat that had been placed using a hand-held GPS unit.

We initially laid out a north-south mapping line, called the *baseline* by archaeologists, parallel to the port (west) gunwale of the wreck. We then laid out a second baseline parallel to and outside the starboard (east) gunwale. Stakes or mapping points then were driven into the beach every 1 meter along the east and west baselines. We next stretched string and fiberglass tapes between the two baselines at 1-meter intervals, using plumb bobs to record the exact locations of the various structural elements that fell along each line. These measurements were then used to create a map of the wreck on a *plane table*, which is a large mapping board that sits on a tripod. Plane tables are old instruments in themselves (the one we used probably dated to the 1920s or 1930s) but still have their uses in ensuring accuracy of a plan map before investigators leave the field. This procedure was particularly crucial in regard to mapping the *America,* as once the wreck went back under water we could not return to check our measurements.

As we began mapping, it became clear that the *America* wreck represented the partial remains of the lower section of a shell-built edge-joined

4.6. Mapping the flatboat interior by SIUC students, 2002.

4.7. Appearance of the intact starboard (right) gunwale prior to mapping. The gunwale is being propped up by stakes so it can be mapped and photographed. John Schwegman, who first found the boat in 2000, is at the far right.

flat-bottomed vessel (Figure 4.8). Structural members still present in 2002 included the aft section of the port gunwale; the virtually intact starboard gunwale; the stern girder, or stern piece; a fragmentary stern plank; three longitudinal stringers, the central one of which consisted of only a small fragment; two cross-ties; and approximately 25 floor planks (Figures 4.8 and 4.9). A pile of displaced bricks along the outboard side of the port gunwale represented the remains of the brick cluster originally within the boat when it was first discovered.[7] Boat elements present in 2000 but no longer present in 2002 included the north end of the broken port gunwale, which had been sawn off and removed by the wreck discoverers.

The wreck represented approximately two-fifths of the bottom of the boat hull (Figure 4.9). The stern was largely intact, with the wreck becoming increasingly fragmentary toward the missing bow. The wreck measured 12 feet (3.7 meters) wide by 44.3 feet (13.5 meters) along the starboard gunwale. The starboard gunwale appeared to be virtually intact, possibly missing only a few inches to a few feet off the northern end. If this interpretation is correct, it indicates that the boat originally measured about 12 feet wide by 45 feet long.

4.8. View of the *America* after removal of fill. The checkered arrow points north in this and other photographs of the wreck. SIU student Jill Aud stands by the plane table used to help map the wreck.

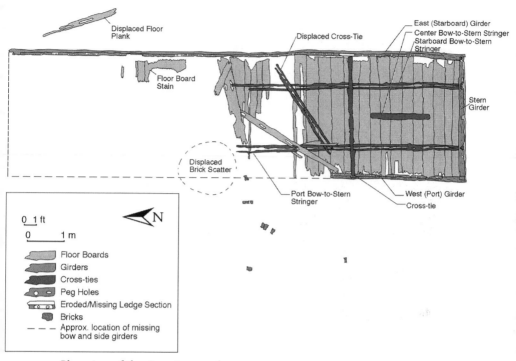

4.9. Plan view of the *America* wreck.

GUNWALES. The two rectangular gunwales consisted of chine-girders split out of a single oak tree (Figures 4.7, 4.10, 4.11, and 4.12). This tree measured at least 45 feet long, based on the length (44.3 feet) of the starboard gunwale. The less intact port gunwale apparently measured about 17.6 feet long when first discovered in 2000. The discoverers cut a 30-inch-long section off the northern end of this gunwale, reducing it to its current length of 15.1 feet (Figure 4.12). The gunwales measured approximately 1 foot high by 2 to 3 inches wide. The smooth outboard sides of the gunwales lacked any visible ax or saw scars. A 1.5- to 2.0-inch-wide groove extended south down the center of the outboard side of the starboard gunwale for approximately 6.25 feet from the broken forward end of the gunwale. Rather than being man-made, this groove has been eroded into the gunwale by the river current running alongside it (Figure 4.10).

A series of ten holes, the center points of which were spaced 4 feet apart, extended the length of the starboard gunwale, while the less intact port gunwale contained two partial and two complete holes (Figures 4.10, 4.11, and 4.12). The holes varied in shape, with those nearest the stern on

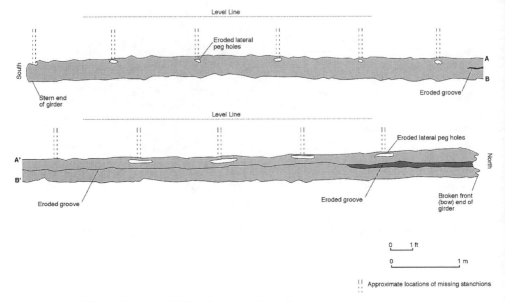

4.10. View of outboard side of east (starboard) gunwale.

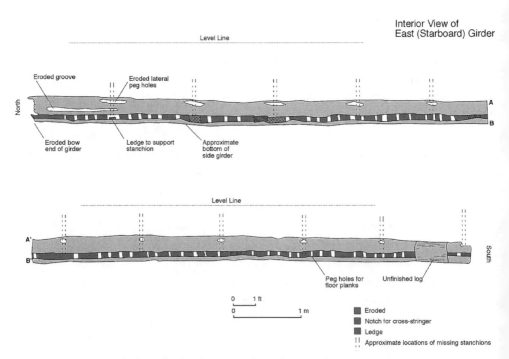

4.11. View of inboard side of east (starboard) gunwale.

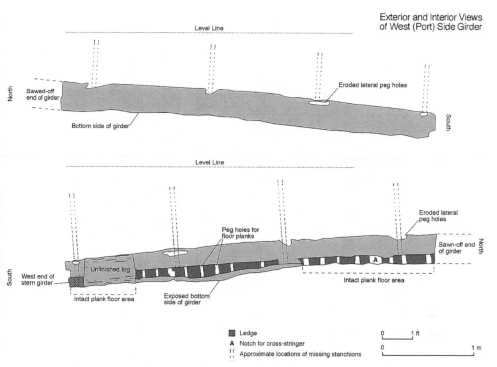

4.12. View of outboard (top) and inboard (bottom) sides of west (port) gunwale.

both gunwales being circular and approximately 3 inches in diameter. The holes became steadily more elliptical toward the forward part of the starboard gunwale, with the most northern hole measuring 18 inches long. This change in shape from the aft to the forward sections of the gunwales is the result of water action and erosion over the years. All of the holes probably measured 1 to 2 inches in diameter when first drilled. The holes on the aft end of the starboard gunwale still retain much of their original circular appearance due to this end of the boat having been buried in the sand (Figure 4.13). The northern end of the starboard gunwale, however, apparently has been sticking up out of the sand for many years. As a result, the current and wave action have eroded the circular peg holes in this part of the gunwale into long ellipses (Figure 4.14). All of these holes once held wooden treenails that attached the lower portions of the stanchions to the gunwales. The wooden planking that formed the sides of the flatboat was then pegged to the upper parts of the stanchions.

The inboard sides of the gunwales consisted of five separate sections. Measuring from the stern and proceeding forward, we found the first of

4.13. Slightly eroded peg hole for stanchion, aft end of starboard gunwale.

4.14. Heavily eroded elliptical peg hole for stanchion at forward end of starboard gunwale.

these sections (0–2 inches) consisted of a 2-inch-wide open space at the ends of the 2-inch-thick gunwales designed to hold the two ends of the stern plank, the aft-most structural member on the boat. The second section (2–8 inches) was similar to the first with the exception of a 1-inch-thick by 4-inch-wide ledge that extended out of the inboard side of the gunwale 7 to 8 inches below the top of the gunwale. This tenon-like ledge overlapped the thinned port end of the stern girder. A single 1-inch-diameter hole that held a wooden treenail had been drilled through the center of the port gunwale ledge into the underlying stern girder, creating a lap joint that held these two members together. A similar hole had been drilled through the starboard gunwale ledge. In this case, however, the hole had been drilled badly off-center and extended partially off the inboard side of the ledge.

In the third section (8–28 inches) the inboard sides of the two gunwales had been left untrimmed (Figures 4.9, 4.11, 4.12, and 4.15), thus retaining the original rounded shape of the log from which they had been cut. Both gunwales measured approximately 6 inches thick (maximum) in this area, indicating that the tree from which they had been cut must have measured about 1 foot in diameter. This section of the two gunwales may have been left untrimmed to strengthen the aft part of the gunwales near the stern of the vessel.

The fourth section (2.3 to 42 feet on the starboard gunwale, 2.3 to 15.1 feet on the port gunwale) formed the major part of the two gunwales. The major feature in this area consisted of a 3-inch-thick by 4-inch-wide ledge to which the floor planks and side plank stanchions originally would have been attached. On the inboard sides of the two gunwales, this ledge was created by cutting a 1-inch-deep by 5-inch-wide rabbet out of the gunwale bottom and an 8-inch-deep by 4-inch-wide rabbet out of the gunwale top. The inboard edges of the two ledges retained the untrimmed rounded appearance of the

4.15. Aft end of starboard gunwale showing untrimmed section of gunwale.

4.16. Peg holes on inboard ledge for attachment of floor planks to port gunwale.

log from which the gunwales had been cut. The two ledges varied in state of preservation, but both were characterized by numerous eroded, broken, and missing sections. The starboard gunwale ledge, however, still contained 54 peg holes that once helped to attach the floor planks to the gunwale bottoms (Figure 4.16). The much smaller port gunwale, in contrast, contained only 16 such holes. The peg holes generally measured about 2 inches in diameter, occurring at regular 3- to 6-inch intervals in the more intact sections of the starboard gunwale. This spacing suggests that two treenails placed 6 inches apart may have been inserted through each plank to attach these members to the gunwale bottoms. The 2-inch diameter for the peg holes represents an eroded diameter, with the original diameter probably being closer to 1 inch.

This section of the gunwale also contained rectangular mortises for the insertion of the cross-ties. The starboard gunwale contained three fragmentary mortises, the center points of which were spaced 11 feet apart, while the port gunwale contained a single intact mortise. The intact mortise measured 7 inches long (possibly 6 inches originally) by 2 inches high by 3 inches deep. The mortise had been cut into the inboard side of the ledge, leaving one-half inch of the ledge intact above and below the mortise.

The final section extended 42 to 42.3 feet along the starboard gunwale. An irregular 15-inch-long eroded piece of wood extended 3 inches from the inboard side of the gunwale in this area (Figure 4.9). This piece of wood may represent a badly eroded remnant of the untrimmed log from which the gunwale was cut, similar to that in the second section near the stern. If our interpretation of this piece of wood is correct (and it is not clear it is), it indicates that the forward ends of the gunwales were similar in appearance to the aft ends. Also, if we assume the untrimmed sections of the gunwales near the bow were similar in length to those at the stern, the overall length of the bottom of the *America* hull was approximately 45 feet.

STERN GIRDER. The oak stern girder consisted of a squared timber that measured 11.5 feet long by 4 inches high by 7 inches wide (Figures 4.9 and 4.17). The intact port end of the stern girder decreased in width to 6 inches at about 4 inches from the inboard side of the port gunwale. At this same point the stern girder decreased in thickness to 2 inches, creating a 4-inch-long by 2-inch-wide rabbet that extended under the gunwale rabbet. This type of joint, in which two rabbets overlie each other, is called a rabbet, or lap, joint. A 1-inch-diameter hole drilled through the centers of the two overlapping members would have contained a treenail to connect the gunwales and stern girder to each other. As noted in the description of the gunwales, however, the hole intended to connect the starboard gunwale rabbet to the stern girder rabbet on that side of the boat was drilled badly off-center, barely connecting these two members.

4.17. View of stern showing stern girder, stern plank, and longitudinal stringers.

4.18. Close-up of stern girder showing rectangular slot for center longitudinal stringer.

The bottom of the stern girder contained three rectangular slots spaced approximately 3 feet apart (Figures 4.18 and 4.19). As noted in the description of the longitudinal stringers, these 7-inch-wide by 2-inch-high slots held the aft ends of these stringers. The slots extended completely through the stern girder. The stringers extended into these slots but ended approximately 2 to 3 inches short of the back of the stern girder. This gap between the ends of the stringers and the back of the girder provided a space for the bases of the stanchions to which the stern planking was attached.

Other features on the stern girder included a series of grooves and drilled peg holes on the top side of this member (Figure 4.17). The grooves were interpreted as erosional features, although it is possible that some of them originally could have been drilled holes. Three of the four approximately 1-inch-diameter holes drilled into the top of the stern connect to the lateral holes drilled through the stern plank into the rear side of the girder. The fourth, to the starboard side of the center stringer, misses connecting with another lateral peg hole by only a few inches. It is unclear as to what the purpose of connecting these sets of peg holes could have been. If anything, such a connection would appear to have weakened the lateral treenails connecting the stern plank to the stern girder. As this board was still present, however, it obviously did not. Another possibility is that these holes connected some now-missing structural member to the top of the stern girder. What this object could have been is again unknown.

Plan View of Stern

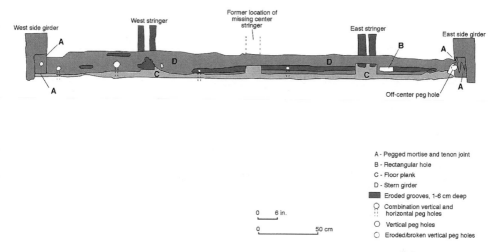

West side girder

West stringer

Former location of
missing center
stringer

East stringer

East side girder

A
D
C

B
A

D
C

Off-center peg hole

A

A

A

A

A - Pegged mortise and tenon joint
B - Rectangular hole
C - Floor plank
D - Stern girder
▮ Eroded grooves, 1-6 cm deep
⚲ Combination vertical and
   horizontal peg holes
○ Vertical peg holes
◔ Eroded/broken vertical peg holes

0   6 in.

0   50 cm

4.19. View of top of stern girder.

STERN PLANK. The *America* stern plank was the only remaining part
of the vessel superstructure (Figures 4.17, 4.20, and 4.21). This plank measured 136 inches long by 11.8 inches high by 1 inch thick. I suspect that it
originally measured 140 inches long by 12 inches high. A 140-inch length
for this board, when added to that of the 2-inch-thick gunwales, results in a
144-inch, or a 12-foot, width for the *America*. The stern plank was attached
to the stern girder by drilling a series of 1-inch-diameter holes slightly above
the bottom edge of the plank and then inserting wooden treenails into
these holes. The spacing between these holes is irregular, and it is possible
that we failed to identify some masked holes that contained the remnants
of broken-off wooden treenails. Three pairs of 1-inch-diameter holes also
had been drilled into the stern plank at 3-foot intervals for the attachment
of the stanchions. These pairs of holes originally consisted of one hole
above the other approximately 6 inches apart. Water action, however, had
eroded three of the holes into long ovals measuring up to 14 inches long,
while two were broken or missing. The single intact hole (the bottom hole
in the central group of holes) measured 1 inch in diameter.

FLOOR PLANKS. The oak floor planks of the *America* lay transversely
across the bottom of the vessel (Figure 4.9). Each plank originally had been

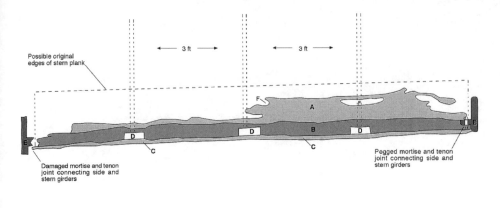

View of Stern Interior

A - Damaged stern plank
B - Stern girder
C - Floor plank
D - Mortise holes for stringer tenons
E - Side girder cross-sections
F - Eroded lateral peg holes
⁞ - Former locations of stanchions

4.20. View of stern interior showing stern girder and stern plank.

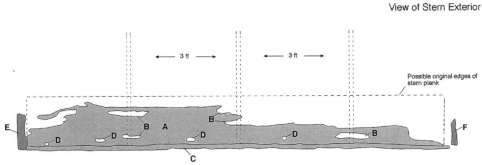

View of Stern Exterior

A - Damaged stern plank
B - Eroded lateral peg holes for attaching stanchions to stern plank
C - Floor plank
D - Lateral peg holes for attaching stern plank to stern girder
E - Cross-section of intact west side girder
F - Cross-section of damaged east side girder
⁞ - Former locations of stanchions

4.21. View of stern exterior showing stern plank, floor plank, and gunwales.

attached to the bottoms of the gunwale ledges by two wooden pegs inserted through holes drilled through the plank ends. The planks appear to have measured 12 feet long by 1 foot wide by 1 inch thick. The exact length of the planks is uncertain, as all of the plank ends were deteriorated. Large elliptical holes in the displaced planks in the forward part of the wreck represent the badly eroded remains of circular peg holes that once attached the floor planks to the stringers. Water action over the years eroded these small (probably 1-inch-diameter) holes into long ovals that in some cases measured over 20 inches in length.

LONGITUDINAL STRINGERS. The *America* wreck contained three longitudinal fore-and-aft stringers (Figure 4.9). These oak stringers, which originally connected to the bow and stern girders as well as the cross-ties, helped hold the flatboat together. They also added support to the floor planks to which they were connected by wooden pegs. Holes were drilled through the floor planks into the stringers, with each stringer being connected to an individual floor plank by two treenails.

The center points of the *America* stringers were spaced approximately 3 feet from each other and from the inboard sides of the upper part of the two gunwales. The starboard and port stringers measured 21.7 and 22.1 feet long, respectively, while the center stringer consisted of a 5.6-foot-long fragment near the stern. In addition, an approximately 9.8-foot-long broken section of the starboard stringer lay at a 45-degree angle across the wreck north of the first cross-tie (Figures 4.8 and 4.9). This section still had been attached to the north end of the starboard stringer at the time of the 2000 investigations.[8] Water action and driftwood slamming into the wreck over the next 1.5 years apparently resulted in this piece being snapped off and shoved into the aft section of the vessel. The starboard and port stringers varied in height from 3 to 4 inches, while the center stringer measured 2 inches high by 4.5 inches wide. Width for the starboard and port stringers varied between 5 and 7 inches. The starboard and port stringers consisted of crudely trimmed saplings that exhibited numerous knots and other surface imperfections. The broken forward, or north, ends of both stringers ended in long split ends (Figure 4.9). The stringers became increasingly solid as they approached the stern but still exhibited the effects of erosional damage in the form of a 1-inch-wide by 1- to-2-inch-deep erosional groove that ran down their centers. This feature appears to have formed as water action eroded the individual peg holes within the stringers into a groove, ultimately breaking through and splitting the northern ends of the stringers into two separate sections. The center stringer was *not* grooved, nor did we identify peg holes in the floor planks to the north and south of this fragment. This finding may indicate that the center stringer was not pegged to the floor for its entire length or, more likely, that we failed to identify the small mud- and wood-filled peg holes associated with this stringer within the floor planks during our 2002 documentation of the wreck. Some indication that at least part of the center stringer was pegged to the floor planks was provided by a large out-of-place floor plank east of the displaced brick pile within the wreck. This plank, the east end of which still touches the starboard gunwale, clearly has a set of two eroded peg holes (one partial and one complete) where it formerly attached to the center stringer (Figure 4.9).

The aft ends of the starboard and port stringers had been thinned in height to 2 inches for their final 6 inches of length, allowing them to fit into rectangular 2-inch-high by 6-inch-wide slots cut into the bottom of the stern girder (Figures 4.9 and 4.22). After they were inserted into these slots, the stringers were attached to the stern girder by driving a single treenail through their tenons.

CROSS-TIES. The *America* cross-ties consisted of two roughly trimmed oak saplings, one lying in its original position 11 feet forward of the stern

4.22. Position of east-west cross-tie over starboard longitudinal stringer.

girder and the other lying at an angle across the aft part of the wreck (Figure 4.9). The latter tie still lay in its original position when the boat was discovered in 2000[9] but had been knocked out of place by the current and driftwood prior to the start of the 2002 SIUC investigations. The ties appear to have been spaced 10.8–11 feet apart. This estimate is based on not only the distances between the center points of the mortises within the gunwales that once held the ends of the cross-ties but also the distance of the remaining in-place cross-tie from the stern girder.

The cross-ties measured approximately 3 to 4 inches high by 6 inches wide (Figure 4.23). These very crudely trimmed timbers retained a large part of their original surface, including knots, although parts of the sides and tops had been roughly trimmed into shape. Three rectangular slots measuring approximately 6 inches long by 2 inches high had been cut into the bottom sides of the two stringers to enable them to be placed over the three longitudinal stringers (Figure 4.24). The cross-ties ended in 4-inch-long by 6-inch-wide by 1-inch-thick tenons that fit inside the mortises within the gunwale ledges (Figure 4.25). Each tenon contained a single 1-inch-diameter drill hole 2 inches from the end of the tenon. A wooden treenail inserted into the drill hole attached the cross-tie to the gunwale ledge.

4.23. Position of cross-tie over starboard and port longitudinal stringers.

4.24. Slot in cross-tie for center longitudinal stringer.

4.25. Rectangular mortise in port gunwale for cross-tie tenon.

STANCHIONS. The now-missing planking that formed the sides of the *America* originally would have been attached to wooden uprights, or stanchions, set in the gunwales and the bow and stern girders (Figures 2.8–2.10, 3.1, 4.20, and 4.21). None of these stanchions remained at the time of the 2002 SIUC investigations. When the boat was first discovered in 2000, however, the base of a single stanchion remained in place along the stern of the vessel.[10] This approximately 1-foot-high broken stanchion was set immediately behind the aft end of the port stringer in the approximately 2- to 3-inch space between the end of this stringer and the stern plank. The stanchion unfortunately was not measured before it washed away, and its exact size is unknown. From a photograph taken during the 2000 investigations that shows the stanchion still in place, however, it was estimated to be twice as thick as the 1-inch-thick stern plank. It also appears to have been the same width (6 inches) as the longitudinal stringer that lay immediately north of it. In sum, the boat stanchions, at least along the stern, appear to have consisted of 2-inch-thick by 6-inch-wide uprights of unknown length. It is unclear from the photograph whether the stanchion was set completely within the space behind the end of the stringer or whether it had a tenon or dovetail end. I suspect but cannot prove that it had one of these two types of end—tenon or dovetail—to help hold it in place.

UNIDENTIFIABLE BOAT PART. This 6.5-foot-long piece of wood lay at a diagonal across the starboard side of the stern section of the *America* at the time of the 2000 investigations. The two ends of this timber reportedly rested "on the ledge of the [starboard] side [gunwale] and the top of the stern [girder]."[11] A photograph taken at the time, however, shows the aft end of this timber lying very near but not on top of the stern girder. It also shows the timber lying on top of the starboard longitudinal stringer. Schwegman suggested that this timber "may have supported the steering mechanism or been a brace" for the starboard stern corner.[12] This timber was removed at the end of the 2000 investigations and currently is at SIUC.

This roughly squared timber measures approximately 6.6 feet long by 3 inches wide with slight knots projecting out of the sides. One end tapers to a 6-inch-long point, while the other appears to be incomplete. Two half-moon-shaped partial 1- to 1.5-inch-diameter holes are spaced 67 inches apart on one side of the timber. One hole is approximately 5.5 to 6.5 inches from the pointed end, while the other is 3.5 to 5 inches from the other end. What may be worn or slightly broken areas are on the side of the timber opposite both holes.

I could not determine the purpose of this timber. It appears to have fallen into the stern section from elsewhere rather than representing a brace or part of the steering mechanism. Although the 6-foot length of the main part of the timber falls within the size range of a flatboat stanchion, it lacks the drill holes needed to attach the side planking. The presence of two partial holes along one side of the timber suggests that wooden treenails may have been driven in next to the timber to wedge it against another structural member. The motion of the boat may have caused the timber to rub against these treenails, eventually wearing two semicircular holes into one face. Even if this interpretation is correct, it still remains unclear why it would have been necessary to wedge one structural member against another or what part of the boat this timber originally came from.

5. Spoons, Pots, Caulking Irons, and Wood Samples: The *America* Artifacts

*T*he artifacts described in this chapter include those recovered by John Schwegman during his initial investigations (Figures 5.1–5.3) as well as those found by us in 2002 (Figure 5.4). Items found by Schwegman within the boat hull in 2000 included an iron felling axe, pewter button, boat caulking iron, clasp knife blade, 3 iron tubes, 2 bone-handled utensils, 3 pewter spoons, and 17 sherds forming part of a single redwaremilk pan.[1]

The SIUC artifact collection consists of 2 metal buttons, a bone-plated utensil handle, 3 redware sherds, 3 pieces of olive green bottle glass, a light green glass vial neck, 3 handmade iron spikes, and 73 whole and broken

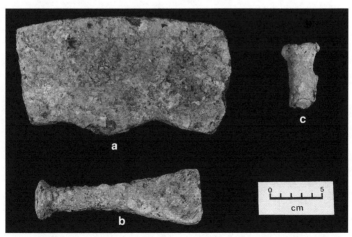

5.1. Artifacts from the *America* site: (a) axe, (b) caulking chisel, (c) iron cylindrical object.

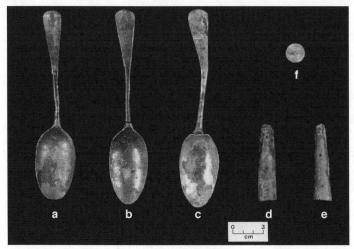

5.2. (a–c) Pewter spoons, (d, e) bone-plated utensil handles, and (f) button from wreck.

5.3. (a) Rim and (b) base of redware milk pan.

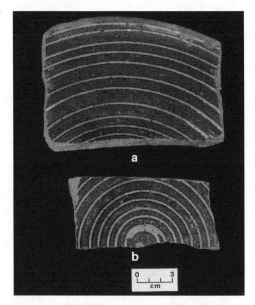

bricks. We recovered small items from within the wreck by taking the fill to the edge of the Ohio River and using water to screen it (Figure 5.5). We also used a metal detector to sweep the beach around the *America* in a search for artifacts that may have fallen out of the boat when it wrecked (Figure 5.6). The Ohio River beach in the area of the wreck is literally covered with washed-in debris, and most of the items we recovered, such as clam musseling hooks, clearly postdated the wreck (Figure 5.7).

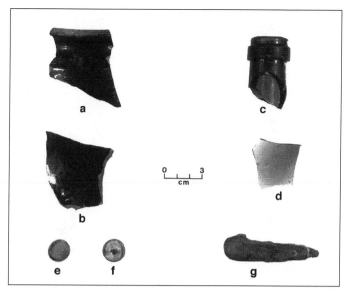

5.4. (a, b) Redware jar parts, (c, d) bottle parts, (e, f) buttons, and (g) bone-plated utensil handle recovered during the SIUC investigation of wreck.

5.5. Water screening of the wreck fill to recover artifacts, 2002. An Ohio River barge, which is the modern-day version of a flatboat, is passing in the background.

5.6. SIUC team sweeping
the beach that surrounds
the wreck with a metal
detector to recover items
that once may have been
contained within the boat.
The wreck excavation is in
the background.

In 2000 John Schwegman removed a section of the port gunwale, which he
submitted to Dr. Charles Ruffner at SIUC for tree-ring dating that could
provide information about the age of the wreck. The SIUC team also removed six small wood samples from various sections of the wreck to learn
about the type of wood used in the construction of the boat. The results of
these analyses follow the artifact descriptions, below.

The wreck also contained a large number of unidentifiable rusted iron
fragments as well as washed-in late-nineteenth- to twentieth-century artifacts identical to those that littered the beach in the area of the wreck. These
items are not discussed further in this book, but information regarding
them can be found in the technical report that we submitted to the Illinois
Historic Preservation Agency (IHPA) in 2003.[2]

5.7. Recovery of an iron "clamming" hook used to catch freshwater mussels that postdated the wreck by at least one hundred years. Most of the items found with metal detection were of similar age.

Artifacts

Felling Axe

The iron axe head found in 2000 within the boat consists of a single-bit polled axe with a rectangular straight-sided cross-section that tapers gradually to a biconvex, or "knife," bit (Figure 5.1a). The axe head measures 1 inch thick at the poll and 3½ inches high at both the poll and bit ends. It is 7¼ inches long from poll to bit. Iron flanges or lugs extend down for approximately ½ inch on both sides of the eye to protect the now-missing axe handle. The top of the axe is slightly curved down rather than expanding, with the downward curvature increasing near the bit end. The bottom of the axe, however, expands out and down from immediately in front of the eye to form the bottom of the excurvate ("curving outward") blade edge. Fragmentary remains of the wooden handle are still visible within the eye socket.

The *America* axe head is similar in style to a "Jersey" or "Kentucky" felling axe, which had an extended eye flange or lug to protect the handle.[3] A virtually identical late eighteenth-century axe is illustrated by Neumann and Kravic, who define axes of this type as "larger camp axes."[4] Kauffmann's note that this axe form was developed by at least 1789 is based on its illustration in a Philadelphia newspaper advertisement of that same year.[5] The manufacture of Jersey-pattern axes continued throughout the nineteenth and twentieth centuries. The *America* axe also exhibits the biconvex knife-shaped bit of a felling axe, as opposed to the chisel bit of a broad axe. Broad axes, which have one flat and one rounded side as well as chisel-edged bits, are used for trimming logs into shape, while felling axes generally are used for cutting down trees and chopping wood.[6] As such, the crew of the *America* may have used this particular axe to chop firewood for the flatboat hearth or to cut away any submerged or floating trees and logs that the America might have encountered on its voyage.

Caulking Iron

Caulking irons are chisel-shaped flared-bit iron tools used to drive a caulking material known as "stranded oakum" into the seams of a wooden ship to make it watertight.[7] The *America* caulking iron has a flattened disk-shaped poll, round shaft, and flared working end that terminates in a knifelike bit (Figure 5.1b). The total length is 6 inches, while the rounded shaft and flattened circular poll measure ¾ inches and 1¼ inches in diameter, respectively. The two sides of the blade taper steadily in thickness from ¾ of an inch at the blade-shaft junction until they meet to form the bit edge of the tool. The blade measures 2 inches wide from side to side at the bit edge. Salaman identifies this particular type of caulking iron as a set iron, the "most ordinary" or "most common" type of caulking iron.[8]

The first step of caulking a large wooden vessel with caulking irons such as that found in the *America* involved laying oakum (a stringy, loose hemp fiber created by taking apart old ropes), which had been twisted into a strand, into the open seam. A wooden caulking mallet, which looked like a croquet mallet, was then used in combination with the set iron to drive the oakum into the seam (Figure 5.8). The oakum was then further compressed into the seam and sunk below the surface through use of a "making iron," which had a blunt or creased bit edge. The seam was then filled with pitch.[9] The seams of smaller vessels could be sealed in a one-step process using a single set iron. This involved twisting the "oakum into a loose cord of a size that will fit nicely into the seam," dipping it piece by piece into the pitch until it was saturated, then driving "it into the openings hard and firm with sharp . . . blows of [the caulking] chisel and mallet."[10]

5.8. Late eighteenth- to early nineteenth-century caulking mallet of the type that would have been used in combination with the caulking iron recovered from the *America. Personal collection, Mark Wagner.*

Caulking irons appear to have been part of a basic boat maintenance tool kit carried by most Ohio and Mississippi River travelers. River guide Zadok Cramer urged all such travelers to protect themselves from danger by acquiring "a few pounds of oakum, together with a mallet and caulking iron. These precautionary provisions might sometimes be the means of saving . . . a loading worth many thousands of dollars."[11] Hitting obstructions such as rocks or submerged trees could cause the flatboat floor planks to separate, requiring the seams to be caulked and filled with pitch once more to keep the boat afloat. Floor planks also could separate if they dried out as a consequence of the boat running aground or being stranded due to an unexpected drop in the river. Cramer also advised travelers to make certain that their boat was properly caulked before starting out, noting that "if she has been long built, her timbers and planks may have shrunk, and the caulking got loose." He also noted that the majority of flatboats apparently were "seldom caulked above the gunnel [variant of *gunwale*] joint," a procedure that he thought "a great error."[12]

Metal Clothing Buttons

The *America* produced three metal clothing buttons. These included a white-metal coin-shaped button found by the initial discoverers of the wreck[13] and two brass buttons recovered by the SIUC investigators. The front of the white-metal button contains a circular thistlelike stamped design, while a mold line extends across the otherwise plain back of the button (Figure 5.2f). The button has a soldered shank that lacks a foot ring. This 19.5-millimeter-diameter (¾ inch) button is similar in appearance to the "Type 11" button defined by an archeologist named Stanley South on the basis of his excavations at historic sites in the southeastern United States.[14] The Type 11 button was manufactured during a long period (ca. 1726–1865), which makes it of little use in trying to precisely date the age of the wreck.

The two brass buttons recovered by us in 2002 are identical in size and appearance (Figure 5.4e, f). Both have soldered brass or copper shanks set in a foot ring. Cleaning of the button backs revealed that one contained a badly eroded set of letters that appeared to represent the word "GILT." Both 0.78-inch-diameter (19.9 mm) buttons have flat fronts decorated with a simple concentric circle, a slight chamfered edge between the face and the side, and a flat side oriented at a right angle to the button face. Button height, measuring from the front to the back ends of the sides, is 2.3 mm (0.09 inch). The buttons are C-shaped in profile, as opposed to the typical flat or coin-shaped profile of most late eighteenth- to mid-nineteenth-century brass buttons.

Bone-Plated Handles

The flatboat discoverers recovered two bone-plated utensil handles,[15] while we recovered a third example. The first two handles are similar in appearance, each consisting of two bone grips fixed to an iron bolster plate by three iron pins (Figure 5.2d, e). Both handles are rounded to oval in cross-section and are identical in length (3 inches) and maximum width (0.55 × 0.7 inches). One handle has three very small parallel incised lines between the two pins nearest the rear end, while the other is plain. The incised lines, which are perpendicular to the long axis of the handle, appear to be incidental cut marks rather than an intentional decoration. The tapered shapes of the handles suggest that they once held spoons or forks, with the latter judged more likely.

The handle recovered during the 2002 excavations measures 2.5 inches long by 0.45–0.74 inches wide (Figure 5.4g). It consists of two bone plates fixed to an iron bolster by two iron pins. The proximal end of the handle swells out to form a rounded end similar to that of a swell-ended knife or fork. The distal end of the iron bolster expands out to form two projections that may represent the remains of broken fork tines. This handle is very similar in overall appearance to swell-ended bone-plated two-tined forks recovered by archaeologists from a late eighteenth-century context at a site called Fort Michilimackinac in the lower Great Lakes region.[16]

Clasp Knife

This knife type is represented only by a small section of the bolster plate (not shown). The object was 1.1 inches long by 0.55 inches wide. The finished rounded end of the plate measures 0.5 inches long, while the broken blade end measures 0.65 inches long. This blade originally would have been folded back into a bone-plated handle just as a modern pocket knife operates.

Pewter Spoons

John Schwegman's 2000 investigations recovered three complete pewter spoons from the wreck (Figure 5.2a–c). Two of the three pewter spoons measured approximately 7.5 inches long, while one measures about 8 inches long. All three had ovate bowls and long tapered stems that ended in rounded ends. All three also contained a raised loop decoration on their front side at the proximal end of the stem. Two of the spoon bowls exhibited faint lines along their long axes that appeared to be the result of milling. All three contained maker's marks on the stem backs, only one of which could be definitely identified. The legible mark consisted of the partial word "—NSEND" contained within a banner or scroll at the top of the mark. This is part of the mark "TOWNSEND/&/COMPTON," an 1801–1811 British pewter company in London, England.[17]

A second spoon contained the capital letters "IP" within a circular or oval cartouche. This mark could not be matched with published examples of those of late eighteenth- and nineteenth-century British and American pewter makers. The "I" in this mark, however, most likely stands for "Iohannes" or John. As such, it is possible that this mark is that of John Perry, a London pewter maker who also used the letter "I" to stand for the letter "J" in the word "John." Two men named John Perry are known to have manufactured pewter in London, England, during the periods 1765–1801 and 1804–1818. The initials on the *America* pewter spoon, however, differ from the two known marks employed by the men named John Perry. The earlier John Perry spelled out his entire name (IOHN/PERRY), while the second used the first letter of his first name in combination with the full spelling of his last name (I/PERRY) within an oval cartouche. Cotterell suspected that these two different marks might be those of a single John Perry at different points in time.[18] If so, it is possible that Perry used yet a third mark containing his initials (IP) on smaller items such as spoon handles. The death date (1818) of John Perry also is in general agreement with the suggested date range (1800–1830) of the *America* wreck.

This same spoon had a large "X" stamped on the back of the stem. The "X" symbol, if used by a British pewter manufacturer of the seventeenth or eighteenth century, denoted "extraordinary" quality and could not be used without government permission. Late eighteenth- and nineteenth-century American pewter makers, however, as well as Victorian-era British pewter manufacturers indiscriminately applied this mark to lower-quality pewter objects that they knew did not meet the British government standards for high quality.[19]

Redware Ceramic Vessels

The flatboat produced 20 redware sherds representing the remains of at least three separate vessels. Redware is a ceramic type used in the late eighteenth through early nineteenth century to make pots, crocks, pans, and other items. The term "redware" comes from the color of the vessels, although sometimes this red is hidden by a brown glaze. Unglazed redware is similar in appearance to a modern flowerpot.

The most intact redware vessel recovered from the *America* consisted of a milk pan found in 2000 (Figure 5.3a, b). Illustrations of very similar milk pans dating to the early 1800s can be found in antique guides.[20] The 2.5-inch-high *America* milk pan consisted of ten rim and seven body fragments, some of which had smoke-blackened exterior surfaces. The pan had a 7-inch-diameter (interior) flat base, slanted walls, and a plain flattened lip that slanted outward to meet the rear wall of the vessel. The vessel opening measured 1 foot wide. Thickness measurements for this vessel included a rim thickness of 0.42 inches, body thickness of between 0.35 and 0.37 inches, and a basal thickness that varied from 0.26 to 0.30 inches.

The vessel interior, with the exception of the lip, was covered with a manganese-flecked clear lead glaze, while the exterior was unglazed. Both the interior and exterior were brown; a fresh break revealed that the vessel had a yellowish red paste under the brown. The paste color probably represents the original color of the now dirty and fire-blackened exterior. It also is possible that the interior glazed surface also had a more reddish appearance than it now exhibits. The generally uniform paste contained some small grit fragments that probably represented accidental inclusions. The vessel interior was decorated with a single line of olive yellow slip that formed a series of 18 concentric rings that spiraled in toward the center of the vessel base.

We (SIUC) recovered three additional redware sherds consisting of a small jar rim and two jar or crock body fragments in 2002. The jar rim (Figure 5.4a) and the smaller of the body fragments (Figure 5.4b) are very similar in appearance, suggesting they may once have formed part of the same vessel. Both have dark reddish-brown glazed interior and exterior surfaces as well as reddish-yellow paste. The rim sherd consists of the rim and shoulder of a small jar that had a high rounded shoulder, a short neck, and an extruding rolled rim. The diameter of the vessel mouth was estimated to be approximately 4 inches, indicating that this rim once formed part of a small-mouthed jar. In form (but not color) this rim is very similar to that of an early nineteenth-century redware straight-sided preserve jar illustrated by Ketchum.[21]

The remaining redware body fragment had dark brown and very dark brown glazed exterior and interior surfaces, respectively. The yellowish red paste probably had a more reddish appearance when first made. From its degree of curvature, this body sherd once formed part of the side of a relatively large jar.

Bottle Fragments

We recovered one light green and three olive green bottle fragments from within the wreck and the surrounding beach. Screening of the wreck fill produced one olive green bottle neck (Figure 5.4c), one thin flat olive green body that may be from a "case-style" or square bottle (Figure 5.4d), and one light green vial neck (not shown). Survey of the beach east of the wreck recovered a curved body section to a ¼-inch-thick nineteenth-century olive green wine or brandy bottle. Both of the bottle necks lack mold seams, meaning that they were part of hand-blown bottles that may date to the early 1800s. The flat-topped olive green bottle neck has what archaeological glass researchers call a "champagne-type" bottle neck finish consisting of a wide flat-topped string rim a short distance below the lip (Figure 5.4c).[22] Jones and Sullivan did not assign a date to this finish style but noted that it is distinguished from that of earlier eighteenth-century French bottles by its regular appearance. A photograph of a French bottle with a finish similar to that of the *America* bottle, however, that reportedly came from a 1740–1780 context is illustrated in a book on colonial-period artifacts.[23] Finally, a bottle collecting authority named Cecil Munsey illustrated a wine bottle with this same finish that he dated to about 1800 but provided no information on how he arrived at this date.[24] The lip finish style exhibited by the *America* bottle neck continued in popularity throughout the nineteenth century as indicated by its presence on bottles recovered from 1849–1891 contexts in the American West.[25] In sum, this bottle fragment could be associated with the wreck or it could postdate it by almost 70 years; it is simply impossible to tell.

The light green vial neck recovered from within the wreck has a horizontal flanged lip that slopes inward slightly toward the neck of the bottle. These types of small medicine bottles were very popular in the late 1700s and early 1800s and have been recovered from a number of early nineteenth-century sites in Illinois[26] and elsewhere in the upper South.[27] An archeological bottle researcher named Ron Deiss assigned an end date of the early 1870s for this type of bottle,[28] but we have never seen examples of this type in such a late context in our own excavations. As such, this small broken medicine vial may very well have been contained within the *America* when it wrecked.

Iron Cylinders

Three corroded iron cylindrical objects were recovered from within the wreck. The most complete of them consists of an approximately 2.3- to 2.4-inch-long hollow tubelike object that resembles the socket or handle of a broken bayonet (Figure 5.1c). The cylinder has an exterior (rusted) diameter of 0.9 inches and an interior diameter of approximately 0.7 inches. The diameter of the lip ring varies from 1.1 to 1.25 inches. An irregular 0.15-inch-wide by 0.50-inch-wide irregular opening is present in the center of the tube on one side of the object. This opening appears to lie along a seam line, although the rusted condition of the object makes it difficult to determine for certain. The broken end of the cylinder is completely sealed by a rounded iron object that had been inserted into the cylinder until it wedged snugly against the sides. The end that sticks out of the cylinder is irregular, and it may be that this object also is broken.

This cylinder resembles the socket or handle found on late eighteenth- and early nineteenth-century American and British bayonets.[29] It lacks, however, the L-shaped slot needed to lock the bayonet to the musket barrel. The opening on one side of the *America* cylinder is simply too small and irregular to represent the remains of such a slot, suggesting that this item probably is not a bayonet socket. A more likely possibility is that it represents a broken iron candle socket. These tube-shaped candleholders had iron spikes on either the bottom or sides that could be driven into wood to hold the candle upright. Revolutionary War artifact researchers Neumann and Kravic illustrated a socketed candleholder that had a raised lip, seamed side, and straight spike extending from the bottom, an appearance very similar (with the exception of the spike) to the iron tube recovered from the *America*.[30] It may be that the iron object wedged into the bottom of the *America* iron tube represents the top of a now-missing snapped-off spike.

The other two cylindrical objects are too fragmentary to allow firm identification. It is possible, however, that they also represent the remains of candleholders.

Bricks

A cluster of 24 whole and 49 fragmentary handmade bricks was immediately adjacent to the port gunwale of the boat (Figures 4.8 and 4.9). These bricks originally had been within the wreck but were removed and discarded in a pile next to the wreck as part of the 2000 investigations.[31] The beach surrounding the wreck contained numerous other complete and broken bricks in addition to those in the pile, but it could not be determined whether any of these came from the wreck. The 24 intact bricks are soft-pasted and easily erodable, as opposed to hand-fired modern bricks. Each measures approximately 7 inches long by 3½ inches wide by 2 inches thick.

We believe that these bricks once formed part of a hearth, a platform for a stove, or part of a fireplace chimney within a cabin. Descriptions of flatboat hearths, however, indicate that they primarily consisted of wood-framed sand-filled boxes directly on the floorboards of the vessel. The *America* bricks also show no evidence of scorching or heat-spalling as would be expected of soft bricks that had fires built directly on them. The second possibility is that they represent the remains of a platform for a stove. William Richardson noted in 1815 that he and his fellow travelers had put a stove in their flatboat but provided no details on whether it sat on such a brick platform.[32] Stoves, however, appear to have been more typical of keelboats, a boat type that could be used over and over again, rather than flatboats. The bricks also may represent part of the chimney or backing of a brick fireplace within a cabin similar to the one illustrated by Charles Lesueur in 1826 (Figure 2.10).

Hand-Wrought Iron Spikes

The *America* wreck contained three hand-wrought iron spikes. These included a twisted 9-inch-long, ⅜-inch-thick spike with a handmade head; a 5-inch-long by ⅜-inch-diameter spike; and a 6½-inch-long by ¼-inch-diameter spike. All three had chisel-shaped points, a characteristic that has been suggested to date prior to 1812 by nail researchers working in Louisiana.[33] What these spikes would have been used for is unknown. They may have helped hold together now-missing parts of the *America* superstructure, such as a cabin. It also is possible that they represent river-deposited items within the wreck. That they are early nineteenth-century artifacts, however, strengthens the case that they are indeed associated with the *America* wreck.

Wood Identification

We removed small sections of wood from six parts of the wreck—port stringer, starboard stringer, cross-tie, floor plank, stern girder, and gunwale—after we documented the wreck. We sent these samples to ethnobotanist Dr. Lee Anne Newsome, of Pennsylvania State University, for analysis. Her work indicated that all samples were *Quercus* sp., oak, belonging to the white oak anatomical group. Although it is not possible to specify exactly to the level of species for the oak genus, Dr. Newsome thought that the six specimens might be white oak proper, *Q. alba*.[34]

Dendrochronological (Tree-Ring) Analysis

John Schwegman cut off an approximately 30-inch-long section of the north end of the port gunwale in 2000 and subsequently submitted it to Dr. Charles Ruffner, of SIUC's Department of Forestry, for dendrochronological, or tree-ring, dating. Dr. Ruffner indicated that this type of analysis would require cutting one end of the timber to obtain a clean cross-section. The IHPA granted permission for the cutting of the *America* gunwale fragment following a request from the Center for Archaeological Investigation that the tree-ring analysis be allowed to proceed. Dr. Ruffner conducted the analysis on a volunteer basis, which limited the extent to which he could undertake the time-consuming search for matches between the *America* cross-section and established tree-ring chronologies.

Ruffner found a possible match for the *America* timber with a published *Quercus alba* chronology from Andrew Johnson Woods State Park in southeastern Ohio. The correlation was $r = 0.258529$, significant at the .05 level. The possible match indicated an age range of 1779–1857 for the *America* piece. This cross-section date is approximately three decades later than the maximum age (1830) calculated for the *America* based on the artifacts recovered from the wreck. Several of the artifact types recovered from the wreck, however, have long use periods, and an 1857 date is not impossible. Archaeological tree-ring researchers have noted several factors that can affect the accuracy of dates obtained through oak tree-ring matches, including inaccurate estimates of the number of sapwood rings on shaped timbers, the comparison of imported wood with local chronologies, and the use of a single chronology to date a specimen.[35] Shaped timbers often lack some or all of the sapwood rings that once formed the outer part of the tree. The number of sapwood rings in oak is variable both within and between trees. In some cases, some parts of single trees may contain up to 20 more rings than others. Inaccurate estimates of the number of missing sapwood rings from an archaeological specimen could result in a skewed date. Oak heartwood also may reach the bark in some localized areas rather than being completely surrounded by sapwood. If an archaeologically derived timber contained such a localized area of heartwood, tree-ring dating of the specimen could produce a date much later than that of the actual felling date.[36]

A second problem concerns the compatibility of the *America* gunwale fragment with the southeastern Ohio tree chronology. Archaeological studies in England have revealed variances in sapwood ring numbers between native oak timbers (more) and those imported from Europe (fewer). Tree-ring dating of imported timbers based on sapwood estimates derived from English oaks thus can result in felling estimates too near to the present.[37] The *America* was built and imported into southern Illinois from an unknown point of origin that could have been anywhere from one to several hundred miles from where the boat came to rest. This raises the possibility that, like the problem of dating imported wood in England, comparison of the *America* gunwale fragment to the Ohio tree chronology could result in a skewed date if the boat was constructed outside southeastern Ohio.

The third problem consists of the use of a single tree chronology to date the timber. The high correlation ($r = 0.258529$) between the Ohio chronology and the tree-ring pattern of the *America* timber indicates only that they are similar in appearance; it does not prove that the date is correct. This date must be checked by means of comparison with oak chronologies in other parts of the Ohio Valley. Such an expanded search could result in additional cross-matches that could either support the 1857 date or, conversely, indicate that the boat also could have been constructed at some point between 1801 and 1830, a date range more in agreement with the artifacts recovered from the wreck, including the early 1800s pewter spoons, redware milk pan, and handmade iron spikes.

6. How They Did It: Building the *America*

$\mathscr{T}$he 2002 SIUC investigations of the *America* recovered detailed information regarding the vessel type, age, and construction of this nineteenth-century boat wreck (Figures 4.9 and 6.1). They revealed that the wreck consists of the stern section of a flat-bottomed edge-joined vessel as defined by Greenhill.[1]

The architecture of the *America* agrees with nineteenth-century descriptions of the flatboat vessel type.[2] Some of the physical details of the

6.1. The *America*, August 2002.

America, including chine-girder construction, log stern girder, and plank floor probably also were characteristic of other nineteenth-century lower Ohio River flat-bottomed vessels such as wood yard boats, skiffs, lighters, and horse-powered ferryboats. The *America* differs from illustrations of these shallow draft boats, however, in that it had high plank sides fashioned to stanchions set in the gunwales. As such, the *America* clearly represents the remains of a flatboat, as opposed to one of these other flat-bottomed vessel types.

The archaeological and architectural data indicate that the builders of the *America* followed many of the same steps described in the accounts of nineteenth-century flatboat builders.[3] The construction of the *America* wreck differs, however, in several respects from the details provided in these accounts, especially in regard to the construction of the gunwales and the manner in which the stanchions were attached to these gunwales. Such variation should not be surprising, as flatboats were, for the most part, folk-built craft constructed at a number of locations along the Ohio and Mississippi drainages by boatwrights and small-operation farmers who may have followed different building traditions.

The initial step in the construction of the *America* involved splitting an approximately 26-inch-diameter by 45-foot-long (minimum) oak log into two equal sized chine-girders that measured 13 inches high by 6 inches wide. The curved outer surface of the log became the inboard side of the gunwale, while the straight cut interior surface became the outboard side. Then a 9-inch-deep by 4-inch-wide rabbet was cut into the inboard side of each gunwale with the exception of a 20-inch-long section that extended 8 to 28 inches from the aft end of each gunwale. This 20-inch-long section consisted of the unmodified curved outer surface of the log from which the gunwales had been cut. It is unknown whether similar 20-inch-long unmodified sections were left at the forward ends of the two gunwales, but I suspect that they were. At this point, the gunwales must have been turned over. The builders then cut a 1-inch-deep by 4-inch-wide rabbet in the inboard side of each gunwale that ran the entire length of the gunwales. The combination of upper and lower rabbets resulted in the creation of a 4-inch-wide by 3-inch-thick ledge on the inboard side of the two gunwales, except (*1*) in the area of the 20-inch-long unmodified log section, where it was not present; and (*2*) from 2 to 8 inches at the aft end of each gunwale, where the ledge measured only 2 inches thick. The boatbuilders also cut a series of rectangular mortises that measured 7 inches wide by 2 inches high near the bottoms of the inboard sides of the ledges. Intended to hold the ends of the cross-ties, these mortises had center points spaced approximately 11 feet apart.

The builders then inserted the tenon ends of the cross-ties into the mortises. To do this, they must have set up the gunwales parallel to each other and spaced a little less than 13 feet apart. This configuration would have allowed enough room between the gunwales to insert the tenons of the cross-ties into the gunwale mortises. The cross-ties consisted of straight, crudely trimmed saplings or branches that measured about 4 inches thick by 6 inches wide by 11 feet long. The 4-inch-long tenon ends of the cross-ties were trimmed to 2 inches thick. The bottoms of the cross-ties also contained three rectangular slots that measured approximately 2 inches high by 6 inches wide. Spaced 3 feet apart, these slots allowed the yet to be added longitudinal stringers to pass under the cross-ties. The boatbuilders must have inserted all of the cross-tie tenon ends on one side of the boat into their respective mortises, lined up the opposing tenon ends with the mortises on the other gunwale, then pushed the two gunwales together until the tenon ends met the inboard sides of the gunwales. They then drilled a 1-inch-diameter hole through the ledge into each tenon, attaching the tenons to the gunwale ledge by inserting wooden pegs or treenails into each hole. This combination of 11-foot 8-inch-long cross-ties and two gunwales each measuring 2 inches wide resulted in a boat width of 12 feet.

The next step involved attaching the stern and bow girders to the boat framework. The dimensions and shape of the bow girder are unknown, as this member was not recovered. Given the boxlike shape of flatboats, however, it probably was very similar in appearance to the stern girder. The oak stern girder consisted of an 11-foot 8-inch–long squared log that measured 4 inches high by 7 inches wide. The two ends of the girder decreased slightly in width to 6 inches for the final 4 inches of their length.

Two modifications to the bottom of the stern girder occurred prior to its being attached to the boat framework. First, tenons were created at the two ends of the girders by cutting 2-inch-deep by 4-inch-long by 6-inch-wide rabbets at each end. Second, rectangular slots intended to hold the longitudinal stringer ends were cut into the girder at approximately 3-foot (center point) intervals. These 7-inch-wide by 2-inch-deep notches extended completely across the girder. Once these steps had been completed the two tenon ends of the stern girder were laid on top of the 1-inch-thick ledge 2 to 8 inches from the ends of the two gunwales, forming a lap or rabbet joint. The drilling of a 1-inch-diameter hole through the center of the port side lap joint and the insertion of a treenail into this hole then completed the connection of the port gunwale to the stern girder. On the starboard side, however, the hole was drilled off-center, barely connecting the inboard side of the starboard gunwale to the stern girder.

The boatbuilders then attached the oak longitudinal stringers to the boat framework. These stringers consisted of approximately 4-inch-wide by 6-inch-high trimmed saplings that ran the length of the boat (Figure 6.1). As noted above, these stringers were placed on 3-foot centers. The stringers were trimmed to 2 inches in height where they crossed the notches cut into the bottoms of the cross-ties. The 2-inch-high thinned tenon ends of the longitudinal stringers were laid into the notches cut into the bottom of the stern girder and pegged in place using 1-inch-diameter treenails, one to each tenon.

The final step in the construction of the bottom of the *America* hull involved connecting the oak floor planks to the gunwale ledges. Each plank measured approximately 11 feet 10 inches long by 1 inch thick by 12 inches wide. The builders laid the ends of the individual planks within the 4-inch-wide by 1-inch-deep rabbets that had been cut into the inboard sides of the bottoms of two gunwales. The depth of the rabbet cut (1 inch), combined with the 1-inch plank thickness, created a flush bottom across the entire width of the boat. Two holes spaced 4 to 6 inches apart then were drilled through the end of each plank into the gunwale ledge bottoms. Wooden pegs inserted within these holes completed the connection of the plank floor to the gunwales.

The floor planks also must have been connected to the stringers during this construction stage. Nineteenth-century boatbuilders typically inserted treenails into holes drilled through the floor planks and into the stringers to attach these two parts of the boat to each other.[4] A displaced floor plank in the *America* wreck lying slightly southeast of the brick scatter contained three eroded and broken sets of peg holes that corresponded to the starboard, center, and port longitudinal stringers. From the starboard set of holes, it appears as if two holes spaced 6 inches apart were drilled into each plank to attach it to each stringer. As there were three stringers, each plank should contain six holes, or two for each stringer. We did not observe any peg holes, however, along the path of the incomplete center stringer in the aft part of the wreck. Rather than being absent, I believe that these holes probably were filled with snapped-off wooden pegs or mud and that we simply failed to identify them.

The attachment of the floor planks to the bottom of the gunwales and the stringers represented the last step in the construction of the lower part of the *America*. After this procedure the boat undoubtedly was slid into a river or creek and flipped over so that it became right-side up. The boat then would have been towed back to shore so that work on the super-structure could begin. Structural elements added during this construction stage include the stanchions and side planking, interior stanchions (if any), cabin (if present), and supports for the oars and sweeps. The *America* wreck contained information relating to the size, spacing, and placements of the stanchions and planking along the stern and sides of the vessel. It contained no interior features identifiable as the remains of a cabin or shelter, with the exception of the brick scatter. It also lacked any oar, gouger, sweep, or other steering parts or supports.

Stanchions were placed every 3 feet along the stern and every 4 feet along the sides of the *America*. The stern would have contained five stanchions, counting the two at the junctions of the gunwales and stern girder. Three rectangular mortises measuring approximately 2 inches wide by 7 inches long by 2 inches deep were along the outboard edge of the stern girder at the back ends of the lateral slots that held the ends of the longitudinal stringers. The bases of the three innermost stanchions may have been set within these mortises and fixed in place with wooden wedges driven into the slots. It also is possible that these mortises have eroded to their current size and originally were somewhat smaller. If so, the bases of the stern stanchions may have ended in tenons set within these mortises, rather than being full-size.

Strakes, or rows, of oak planks then were attached to the bodies of the stanchions by drilling through the planks and pegging them to the stanchions with treenails. The fragmentary wooden plank along the stern of the *America* revealed that each of the strakes covering the stern of this vessel each consisted of a single plank. These planks appear to have had the same dimensions as the floor planks, measuring 11 feet 8 inches long by 12 inches wide by 1 inch thick. The bottom edge of the bottom plank rested on an approximately 1-inch-wide section of floor plank that extended out from beneath the stern girder. This 1-inch addition in height would have made the top of the bottom strake flush with the tops of the gunwales. The ends of the plank fit within the 2-inch smooth-walled gaps at the aft ends of the gunwales. Two pegs were driven into each plank along each stanchion to hold them in place.

The width and thickness of the side stanchions are unknown, but they may have been similar in size (2 inches thick by 6 inches wide) to the stern stanchions. The builders attached the side stanchions to the gunwales by drilling a 1-inch-diameter hole through the upper part of the gunwale about 6 inches above the inboard ledge into the lower part of each stanchion. The side stanchions also almost certainly had tenon ends set in mortises within the ledge to further hold them in place. In several instances along the badly eroded starboard gunwale ledge below the gunwale drill holes were what appeared to be 1-inch-wide by 2-inch-long mortises set between the outer peg holes of two adjacent floor planks. The bottoms of these possible mortises were set 1 inch below the top of the ledge. If the identification of these features as mortises is correct, it indicates that the side stanchions had 1-inch-long tenons attached to their bases that fit within mortises in the ledges. Given the eroded state of the gunwale ledges, it is possible that the mortises may have been deeper and the tenons consequently longer than the measurements recorded by us. Rather than being set within the gunwale ledge, however, the bases of the stanchions at the junctions of the gunwales and stern girder may simply have rested on the gunwale rabbet or ledge. A possible indication of this is that we did not find a mortise on the ledge below the peg hole at the aft end of the port gunwale. The area below this peg hole instead consisted of the intact lap joint that connected the port gunwale and the stern girder. As such, the base of the stanchion must have rested directly on this joint unless it was set in a mortise cut within a now-missing structural member that once overlay the stern girder and port gunwale joint.

The *America* wreck lacked any evidence of a cabin except for the brick scatter. When the wreck was first discovered this scatter lay along the port gunwale to the north (forward) and south (aft) of the southernmost cross-tie.[5] The jumbled brick scatter extended east from the inboard side of the port gunwale toward the middle of the boat. I believe that rather than representing the remains of a brick hearth, the bricks once may have formed part of a brick fireplace and chimney within a cabin similar to the one drawn by Lesueur (Figure 2.10). This fireplace may have collapsed during the wreck, spilling the bricks eastward into the center of the boat.

7. The Wreck of the *America*

*O*ur 2002 investigations indicated that the *America* wreck represents the remains of an early nineteenth-century flatboat dating to about 1801–1830. The relatively small size of the boat—an estimated 45 feet by 12 feet—also is characteristic of flatboats built before the Civil War. All surviving structural members are made from oak. This use of oak varies from accounts collected from early to mid-nineteenth-century Indiana, Ohio, and Illinois flatboat builders, who used poplar in the construction of the boat gunwales and girders.[1] This difference in wood type may have to do with the early nineteenth-century origin of the *America*. Large straight oak trees measuring 45 feet in length or longer may have been quite common in the Ohio Valley at the time the *America* was built. By the middle to the latter part of the nineteenth century, however, oak trees of this size may have become relatively rare or too valuable to be used in the construction of a one-way boat intended to be sold off and dismantled at the end of its voyage. In response, flatboat builders of the 1830s through the 1860s and later may have shifted away from oak and instead used yellow poplar to build the gunwales and other large structural members of their boats.

The artifacts recovered from the wreck site—redware milk pan, spoons, ax, caulking iron, and so on—represent the personal belongings and tools of the crew. The presence of these types of everyday items within the hull suggests that the *America* was partially or completely submerged after the wreck and that these articles either could not be found under the water or simply were not worth recovering.

Conspicuously absent were any traces of the cargo carried by the *America*. Items typically carried by flatboats that should have left archaeological remnants include barrels with iron hoops; live or butchered animals; and personal possessions such as farming tools, plates and dishes, clothing, sewing items, and weapons. It is possible that cargo items carried by the

America in barrels (if they were present) such as flour and pork simply "floated off in all directions," like the boat wreck witnessed by Timothy Flint.[2] Live animals such as horses, pigs, and cattle also could have jumped off the boat and swum to shore, like the animals on Daniel Trabue's sinking flatboat in 1785.[3]

The cargo of the *America* also could have been salvaged by its crew or that of another boat. The cargo of a stranded or wrecked boat was considered abandoned and fair game for removal if the crew did not remain with the boat to protect their property. Owners often left "a reliable man on each boat to protect the vessel and cargo," in some cases for months, to safeguard the cargoes of flatboats stranded on sandbars by low water.[4] Passing flatboats also could help rescue the crew and cargo of a wrecked boat, taking them and their possessions on board if they had room. Daniel Trabue noted that after his flatboat sank in 1785 the "[o]ther boats came to our assistance with their canoes as quick they could. They did ketch [*sic*] some few of our things that was a sweming [*sic*]" in the water.[5]

The superstructure of the wreck may have been quickly dismantled by passing boat crews or local settlers for the lumber. It also could have broken off and washed away during one of the fall or spring rises of the Ohio River. The gunwales and floor planks, mired in the river bottom, eventually silted over and disappeared from sight for nearly two centuries.

One of the questions we sought to answer through our investigations was, how did the *America* end up wrecked on the Illinois shore? As noted in chapters 1 and 3, we believe it unlikely that pirates attacked the boat, nor does our documentation of the wreck show any evidence that it sank because of violence.[6]

But if the *America* did not sink as the result of an attack or robbery, why did it sink? I believe that the location, orientation, and construction of the wreck indicate that it it is far more likely that it sank from a combination of poor workmanship and natural causes rather than anything else. The wreck is approximately 1 mile below the abandoned early nineteenth-century town of America, which was founded in 1818. This date falls within the suggested range (1801–1830) for the *America*, making it possible that the boat could have stopped at this town. The downstream location of the wreck in relation to the town, however, suggests that the cause of the wreck is not directly associated with the town of America. In other words, the crew of the *America* was not trying to dock at America when it wrecked but already had passed the town when this event happened.

The location of the wreck does agree, however, with river guide Samuel Cumings's 1832 direction for navigating that section of the Ohio River immediately below America:

There is an ugly bar on the right, opposite to New America. When you approach the town, keep over to the left, more than half across the river: When you have passed the town, *incline to the right again*, to avoid the bar at the head of Cash Island.[7]

Cumings gave even more explicit directions in the 1838 edition of the *Western Pilot*, urging downstream navigators to keep to the right side (i.e., the Illinois shore) of the river below New America:

When a mile below town, wear in a little to the right to avoid the bar making off from Cash Island, which lies near the left (Kentucky) shore; *channel to the right opposite this island, near the right (Illinois) shore.* In a little bend there is a large willow tree; this is Cash Bar.[8]

Cumings's navigational instructions indicate that the wreck of the *America*—which is "a mile below [the] town" of America and "a little to the right" side of the river—is in the correct location for a boat that had just passed the America Bar and then swung toward the Illinois shore to begin attempting to pass by the Cash (Cache) Bar (Figure 7.1). In other words, the boat appears to have been proceeding normally downriver when it unexpectedly sank.

The wreck is on the Illinois bank, not on a sandbar in the channel, suggesting that something happened after the *America* passed the America Bar that drove it on shore or that the crew intentionally beached their boat. Natural forces that could have driven the boat ashore include strong currents, high winds, storms, and ice. The boat also could have been damaged by rocks, sawyers, or planters while passing the America Bar, forcing the crew to attempt to land the boat on the Illinois shore.

Two lines of evidence suggest that the crew of the *America* attempted to beach the boat as the result of an accident in the river rather than the boat being wrecked on shore by waves or high winds. The first of these is the orientation of the wreck. The missing bow section of the *America* would point upstream, while the stern forms the downstream end of the boat. This is the correct orientation for a docked or landed flatboat. The pilot of a downriver flatboat attempting to land on the Illinois shore would have

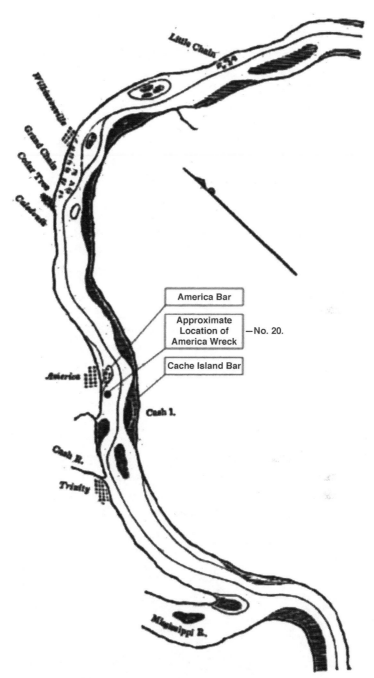

America Bar

Approximate
Location of   —No. 20.
America Wreck

Cache Island Bar

7.1 Location of the *America* wreck relative to the America and Cache Island sandbars. *Cumings 1832.*

taken the boat close into shore. He then would have pulled the handle of the steering oar located above the stern to starboard, causing the "sweep" end of the oar in the water to swing to the port (left) side of the vessel. This would have caused the vessel to begin turning around as the stern completed a gradual swing to port. When the boat was fully turned around—bow facing upstream, stern downstream similar to the *America*—the crew would have tied it to trees along the shoreline to hold it in place.

The *America* is only a partial wreck, consisting of approximately two-fifths of the very bottom of a flatboat hull (Figures 4.8). Any interpretation of the possible cause of the wreck must take into consideration that those portions of the boat most likely to have been damaged in a collision—the forward and bow sections—have not survived. But the condition of the stern section provides one possible explanation for the sinking of the *America*. A difference in preservation exists between the joints connecting the port and stern gunwales to the two ends of the stern girder. The joint connecting the port gunwale to the port end of the stern girder is intact (Figure 7.2), while the starboard gunwale-stern girder joint is rotted and deteriorated (Figures 7.3). The builders of the *America* cleanly drilled the hole connecting the port gunwale tenon to the stern girder tenon through the centers of the two overlapping tenons. A wooden peg, or treenail (now missing), inserted into the hole held these two structural elements together. The peg hole that once connected the starboard gunwale to the starboard end of the

7.2 Close-up of port gunwale-stern girder joint showing centered peg hole.

7.3 Close-up of starboard gunwale-stern girder joint showing off-center peg hole.

stern girder, however, was drilled badly off-center. It falls off the inboard edge of the starboard gunwale tenon, barely connecting that member to the underlying stern girder tenon (Figure 4.15). This poorly connected joint may account for the variance in preservation between the aft ends of the starboard and port gunwales. Water may have been coming in through this bad joint for some time before the boat actually sank, softening and rotting the wood in the area of the joint.

The crew of the *America* may have been unaware of this bad joint if they purchased the boat rather than building it themselves. Based on the location of the aft-most peg hole in the side of the port gunwale, this joint appears to have been hidden from sight beneath the base of one of the upright stanchions to which the side planks would have been attached. River guide Zadok Cramer[9] repeatedly warned flatboat travelers of the shoddy workmanship characteristic of the commercial boatyards on the upper Ohio River, going so far as to call for government inspectors to be stationed at these boatyards to stop the practice of using "injured" or rotten plank in flatboat construction.[10] Even if the *America* had been inspected carefully by such an experienced boatman, however, the bad joint would have been almost impossible to locate unless the inspector removed the stanchion that covered it.

The peg hole connecting the starboard gunwale and stern girder tenons is drilled so far off-center that it is difficult to see how a competent or sober shipwright could have made such an error. The difficulties experienced by Captain Meriwether Lewis in having a keelboat made at a boatyard in Pittsburgh in 1803, however, may shed some light on how this could have happened. Lewis had contracted with a Pittsburgh shipwright to build a keelboat for his expedition to explore the newly acquired Louisiana Territory, west of the Mississippi River. In a letter to President Thomas Jefferson, Lewis complained bitterly of his experiences with this drunken boatbuilder, which delayed the start of the Lewis and Clark Expedition by almost two months:

> [I have] been moste (*sic*) shamefully delayed by the unpardonable neg-
> ligence of my boat-builder. . . . [A]ccording to his usual custom he got
> drunk, quarreled with his workmen, and several of them left him, nor
> could they be prevailed on to return: I threatened him with the penalty of
> his contract, and exacted a promise of greater sobriety in future, which,
> he took care to perform with as little good faith, as he had his previous
> promises with regard to the boat, continuing to be either constantly
> drunk or sick.[11]

Lewis assured the eventual completion of his keelboat by "this incorri-gible set of drunkards" only by monitoring their work on an almost daily basis.[12] If Lewis's experience was typical of the level of sobriety and work-manship found at upper Ohio River boatyards, boats built in these yards very well could have left with off-center holes drilled by careless or drunken shipwrights (Figure 7.4). The owners of such shipyards undoubtedly knew that little chance existed of their ever seeing most of their customers again. Flatboats, after all, were one-way vessels that carried their crews and pas-sengers downstream and *away* from the yards where they had been built, never to return. By the time a family of western-bound emigrants dis-covered at the mouth of the Ohio River that their boat leaked constantly, small likelihood existed of their ever coming back upriver to complain to the boatbuilders. Such may have been the fate of the *America*.

7.4 Early 1800s shipwright driving in wooden pegs, similar to those used to build the *America*, with a mallet that looks like the one in Figure 5.8. *Tabart and Company, Book of Trades, 1807.*

8. What Happened Afterward

$\mathcal{D}$ocumenting a boat wreck on the lower Ohio River is a tricky business. It is a working river with heavy barge traffic. Tugboat-pushed barges piled high with coal and other products travel constantly up and down the river, carrying their cargoes to various river ports in a manner identical to that of nineteenth-century flatboats, keelboats, and steamboats. This heavy traffic, together with the strong current, stirs up the silt-laden water and reduces visibility, making it impossible to see anything beneath the surface of the river. A shipwreck could be only a foot or so beneath the surface of the water, and no one would be able to see it. Divers working in the lower Ohio River on the Olmstead Dam project, a short distance upriver from the *America* wreck, have to work by feel, not vision, as they literally cannot see what is in front of their faces.

In the case of the *America*, even though we knew where it was, we had to wait until the Ohio River dropped to the extremely low level of 11 feet on the Cairo, Illinois, gauge before we could start work at the wreck site. And even then we had only a very limited time to complete this work. The Ohio River drains a large section of the eastern United States, meaning that runoff from heavy rainstorms hundreds of miles away in such far-off locations as Cincinnati and Pittsburgh can raise the river level in the lower Ohio in a few days.

The river level also can be affected by the release of water from upstream dams. Extremely low water on the lower Ohio can affect barge traffic, as such vessels require a certain river depth to avoid getting stuck on the river bottom or sandbars. When low water threatens, the Corps of Engineers releases water from the Tennessee and Cumberland Rivers, which is held behind the dam at Lake Barkley in Kentucky, into the lower Ohio so that barge traffic can continue. The river level can rise several feet or more overnight when dam water is released.

And this is what happened to us in 2002. We started our work at the wreck site on a Thursday (August 7), using a combination of SIUC students and volunteers. At that time, the boat had been out of the water for only a day or so, and the beach around it was still wet and soft (Figure 4.2). The edge of the Ohio River was approximately 30 feet away. We managed to complete most of the documentation of the wreck within a few days. By Tuesday it had begun raining heavily and the Ohio had begun to rise. By Wednesday (one week into the project) the edge of the river was only 10 feet from the boat.

We had contacted the Corps of Engineers and other agencies about obtaining the necessary permits and funding to remove the boat from the riverbank prior to starting work at the site. However, we were unable to obtain these necessities, given the short time frame we were working in. As the river rose, it became clear we needed to cover and stabilize the wreck to stop the approaching current from removing any more of it. We covered the wreck with weed-guard fabric (Figure 8.1), then used a front-end loader to deposit gravel on the fabric to hold it and the wreck in place. This last operation was completed just as the river began covering the boat once again, eight days after it first emerged from the water (Figure 8.2).

The stabilization project was successful in the short run. When I visited the site the following year with an SIUC film crew, the fabric and gravel

8.1. Tarping of the wreck by SIU student Erinn Shockey to prevent it from refilling with river debris and muck prior to being submerged in the Ohio River. The water is closer to the wreck in comparison with earlier photographs, such as Figure 4.6.

8.2. Volunteer Nick Niesrath using a front-end loader to deposit river gravel on the tarp covering the wreck to hold it in place. Within an hour after this photo was taken, the wreck once again was under water.

were still in place (Figure 8.3). During this time I and others continued to discuss, with the various groups that held or claimed jurisdiction, the need to remove the wreck from the riverbank. These groups included members of the local community as well as state and federal agencies such as the Corp of Engineers, the Illinois Historic Preservation Agency, and the state of Kentucky. Citizens of Pulaski County, where the wreck is located, wanted it removed from the riverbank and displayed in their county, but they lacked the funds necessary to preserve and display the wooden framework of the wreck. We were similarly unsuccessful in obtaining a consensus from the state and federal agencies as to what should be done with the wreck if it indeed were removed from the bank. As a result, it remained on the riverbank.

When I once again visited the wreck site in 2007 with SIUC architectural studies professor Bob Swenson, who had been one of our 2002 volunteers, we discovered that the river current had stripped most of the fill out of the wreck and dislodged the intact starboard gunwale, depositing it across the top of the wreck (Figure 8.4). Only by remarkable good fortune had this gunwale caught against another piece of the wreck instead of being washed down the Ohio River and destroyed. We applied for and received emergency funding from the Landmarks Preservation Council in Chicago,

Illinois, to once again stabilize the wreck. Rather than remove the gunwale from the riverbank (which could have resulted in conservation problems if the wood was not immediately treated to preserve it), we used a backhoe to dig a trench on the bank next to the wreck and buried it (Figures 8.5 and 8.6). We then covered the remainder of the wreck with tarp and gravel to stabilize it once again.

Each year the Landmarks Preservation Council assembles a list of the 10 most endangered historic properties in the state to raise public awareness that these sites are in danger of being destroyed. Such properties typically consist of standing structures such as office buildings designed by famous architects that are in danger of being demolished. Bob and I, however, nominated the *America* to this list in late 2007. The Landmarks Preservation Council agreed with this recommendation and listed the *America* as one of the 10 most endangered properties in Illinois in 2008. Despite the public recognition conveyed on the wreck by this dubious honor, we remained unable to obtain funding for the removal and preservation of the wreck. So today it remains on the Ohio River shoreline, where it came to rest some 200 years ago.

The *America*, as the only identified example of an early nineteenth-century flatboat, is an extremely important part of the maritime heritage of

8.3. Film producer Richard Kuenneke inspecting the gravel-covered wreck in 2003 when it was once again exposed during a period of low water.

8.4. Mark Wagner looking at displaced gunwale, 2007.

8.5. Bob Swenson supervising removal of gunwale from on top of the wreck with a backhoe, 2007.

8.6. Burial of the starboard gunwale on the Ohio River shoreline immediately next to the wreck, 2007. Matt Swenson (far left) helps guide the gunwale into the trench.

Illinois and the nation as a whole. It represents a direct physical link to the era when American pioneers and farmers set out on perilous voyages down the Ohio and the Mississippi in rudimentary box-shaped boats, often with no more than a pocket guidebook to warn them of the dangers that might lay ahead. And, as the wreck of the *America* itself demonstrates, many suffered unexpected fates in doing so. My hope in writing this book is that it will bring added public attention to the need to remove the remains of this important piece of our history from the Ohio River shoreline, to stabilize it, and to identify a facility where it may be displayed and interpreted. The story of the *America* would certainly appear worthy of such a happy ending.

Glossary

Notes

Bibliography

Glossary of Boat-Related Terms

aft. Near or toward the stern of a ship or boat.

bow. The forward end of a ship.

chine-girder construction. The splitting of a log into two equal sections to create the side girders of a flat-bottomed boat (Greenhill 1995; Newell 1996).

cross-ties. Also called cross-timbers, girders, and sills. These small-diameter girders ran transversely between the port and starboard gunwales, to which they were attached with wooden treenails. Cross-ties provided stability to the boat framework.

fore-and-aft. Long axis of a ship.

forward. In the direction of the bow.

girders. Shaped logs that formed the sides and ends of the base of flat-bottomed vessels, and to which the floor planks and stanchions were attached. Flatboat builders also used the term *girder* as a generic name for any long piece of shaped timber such as cross-ties and stringers.

gouger. A long oar at the bow of a flatboat.

gunwale. Also spelled "gunnel" and "gunwhale," the two long chine-girders that formed part of the base of a flatboat hull. This is an archaic use of the term *gunwale*, which today is understood to refer to the upper side edge of an open boat.

inboard. Toward the center of a boat.

lap joint. Also called a rabbet joint, the junction formed by two overlapping rabbets.

longitudinals. The fore-and-aft girders in the bottom of a ship. Flatboats had longitudinal stringers that attached to the stern girder, bow girder, cross-stringers, and floor planks.

Source: These definitions are drawn from Greenhill (1976, 1995), Newell (1996), the *Nomenclature of Naval Vessels* (Navy Department 1941), and first-hand accounts collected from nineteenth-century flatboat builders.

mortise. A hole cut in the gunwales or girders to receive the end or tenon of another piece.

oakum. Also called "stranded oakum," a stringy fiber created by taking apart old ropes that were then twisted into strands and used to caulk, or seal, the open seams of a boat. The oakum was hammered into the open seams with a wooden mallet and chisel-like caulking iron, then covered with hot tar pitch to form a watertight seal. Caulking had to be done quickly so the heated tar did not congeal; hence sailors who were in a hurry were said to move "like smoke and oakum."

outboard. Away from the center of a boat; outside the hull.

port. The left-hand side of a ship when looking from aft forward.

rabbet. An L-shaped offset in a member into which another member is fitted so that the two surfaces are flush. Rabbets were cut on the bottom of flatboat chine-girders to hold the ends of the floor planks.

stanchions. Also called studs or studdings, they consisted of evenly spaced wooden uprights set within mortises in the gunwales and stern girder of a flatboat. The planks that formed the sides and stern of the flatboat were attached to the stanchions with wooden pegs.

starboard. The right-hand side of a ship when looking from aft forward.

steering oar. Long oar at the stern of a flatboat.

stern. The aft end of a vessel; farthest from the bow.

strake. A continuous row of wooden planks forming part of the sides of wooden boats. A flatboat that had six-foot-high plank sides composed of 1-foot-wide planks would have contained six strakes of planks.

stringers. Also called keelsons (Newell 1996), sleepers, girders, and sills (Cockrum 1907). These small-diameter longitudinal timbers ran fore-and-aft from the stern girder to the bow girder on flatboats. In combination with the cross-ties, they provided a lattice-like framework for the attachment of floor planks.

sweeps. Long oars attached to the sides of a flatboat.

tenon. The end of a piece of wood cut into the form of a rectangular prism designed to be set into a mortise of like form in another piece.

transverse. At right angles to the ship's fore-and-aft center line.

treenails. Also called trenails, trunnels, pins, and pegs. Short wooden dowels used instead of nails or spikes to secure the planking of early flatboats to the gunwales, stringers, and stanchions.

Notes

1. Introduction

1. Schwegman 2001.
2. Schwegman 2001.
3. Wagner and McCorvie 1992.
4. Rothert 1924.
5. Wagner and McCorvie 2006, 2011.

2. Arks, Broadhorns, and Other Flat-Bottomed Boats

1. Greenhill 1976, 1995:119–120.
2. Greenhill 1976:66.
3. Greenhill 1995:49–51.
4. Newell 1996:19.
5. Dunbar 1915:38, 277.
6. Ambler 1932:33.
7. Dunbar 1915:268–270.
8. White 1991:362–365.
9. Carson 1920:26.
10. Ambler 1932:70.
11. Allen 1990; Scheiber 1969:277–299.
12. Wagner and Butler 1999:41.
13. Anonymous 1806.
14. Brush 1944:93.
15. Allen 1990:61.
16. Allen 1990:64.
17. Havinghurst 1964:32.
18. Scheiber 1969:288–289.
19. Wagner and Butler 1999:41.
20. Greenhill 1995:281; Newell 1996.
21. Brush 1944; Botkin 1955; Phillips 1947.

22. Ambler 1932; Bradbury 1819; Brush 1944; Dunbar 1915; Phillips 1947; Records 1946.
23. Records 1946.
24. Hamy 1968.
25. Hamy 1968: 45, 59.
26. Lewis 1967: plates 68–69, 73; Records 1946:331.
27. Records 1946:330
28. Cramer 1811:34–35.
29. Botkin 1955:311–317; Brush 1944; Carmony 1964:305–322; Phillips 1947.
30. Carmony 1964:309.
31. Brush 1944:150.
32. Botkin 1955:311.
33. Phillips 1947:21.
34. Carmony 1964:311; Phillips 1947:21.
35. Carmony 1964:211.
36. Cockrum 1907:508.
37. Brush 1944:150.
38. Carmony 1964:312.
39. Carmony 1964:313.
40. Carmony 1964:21.
41. Phillips 1947:21.
42. Cockrum 1907:509.
43. Cockrum 1907:509.
44. Carmony 1964:314; Phillips 1947:21.
45. Brush 1944:150.
46. Carmony 1964:314; punctuation added.
47. Brush 1944:150.
48. Botkin 1955:312.
49. Brush 1944:150.
50. Carmony 1964:315.
51. Botkin 1955:311; Phillips 1947:2.
52. Cockrum 1907:509.
53. Salaman 1977:117–118.
54. Neison et al. 1990:46.
55. Carmony 1964:317.
56. Salaman 1977:118.
57. Greenhill 1995:54–55.
58. Cockrum 1907:510.
59. Phillips 1947:21.

60. Botkin 1955:312.
61. Botkin 1955:312.
62. Phillips 1947:21.
63. Cockrum 1907:510.
64. Carmony 1964:317.
65. Brush 1944:232.
66. Phillips 1947:22.
67. Botkin 1955:312.
68. Carmony 1964:317–318.
69. Brush 1944:150.
70. Phillips 1947:22.
71. Botkin 1955:312.
72. Carmony 1964:319.
73. Botkin 1955:212.
74. Brush 1944:150–151.
75. Phillips 1947:22.
76. Carmony 1964:305–322.
77. Carmony 1964:319.
78. Cockrum 1907:510.
79. Shapiro et al. 1990:156–157, 166.
80. Thwaites 1900.
81. Reid and Fuller 1997:37, 42, 50, 67–68, 82, 97.
82. Fuller and Reid 1997: 37, 67, 79, 88.
83. Thwaites 1900:55.
84. Thwaites 1900:89–90.
85. Reid and Fuller 1997:38.
86. Reid and Fuller 1997:88.

3. Dashed to Pieces: Flatboat Wrecks on the Ohio and Mississippi Rivers

1. Anonymous 1806:24.
2. Flint 1968:69.
3. Collot 1826:33.
4. Cramer 1811:33.
5. Cramer 1811:34.
6. Rothert 1924.
7. Wagner and McCorvie 2006.
8. Bancroft 1835:309; Claiborne 1880:531; Rothert 1924:247–251.
9. Hamilton 1933:93.

10. Nuttall 1819:295–296.
11. Corning 1929:33.
12. Rothert 1924:283–306.
13. Anonymous 1943:423.
14. Lincoln 1953:62.
15. Flint 1830a, 1830b.
16. Flint 1830a:103–106.
17. Blair and Meine 1956.
18. Baldwin 1941:118; Prigge 1973; Rothert 1924.
19. Wagner and McCorvie 2006:219–247, 2011:9–14.
20. Alvord 1921:354; Baker 1998:112.
21. Forman 1888:37.
22. Johnson 1980:12–15.
23. Caldwell 1950:272.
24. Schultz 1810:4.
25. Schultz 1810:96–97.
26. Twain 1896:53.
27. Brush 1944:86–87.
28. Brush 1944:88.
29. Ellicott 1803:19–20.
30. Young 1981:35.
31. Thorpe 1845:172–174.
32. Bradbury 1819:209–211.
33. Collot 1826:33.
34. Anonymous 1806:11.
35. Rodney 1997:167.
36. Brush 1944:153.
37. Cramer 1811:133.
38. Brush 1944:153–155.
39. Bedford 1919:55, 57.
40. Anonymous 1806:16.
41. Rodney 1997:141–169.
42. Cramer 1811:37.
43. Ellicott 1803:27–28.
44. Brush 1944:89–90.
45. Richardson 1940:18.
46. Cramer 1811:183–184.
47. Hamy 1968:68.
48. Flint 1968:158–159.

4. Stuck in the Mud: Documenting the America

1. Schwegman 2001:23.
2. Schwegman 2001:25.
3. Schwegman 2001:25.
4. Schwegman 2001:25.
5. Flint 1830a, 1830b.
6. Anderson 1995; Krisman 1993.
7. Schwegman 2001.
8. Schwegman 2001.
9. Schwegman 2001.
10. Schwegman 2001.
11. Schwegman 2001:24, 25.
12. Schwegman 2001:25.

5. Spoons, Pots, Caulking Irons, and Wood Samples: The America Artifacts

1. Schwegman 2001.
2. Wagner 2003.
3. Kauffmann 1972:23; Langsner 1978:44–45; Sellens 2002:33–35; Sloane 1982:31.
4. 1975:26.
5. 1972:25.
6. Sloane 1982:14–15; Langsner 1978:44–45.
7. Cockrum 1907; Neison et al. 1900:45; Salaman 1977:115–116; Sellens 2002:114; Stevens 1976:92–96.
8. 1977:Figure 187/2k; 188; Sellens 2002:114–115.
9. Salaman 1977:117–118.
10. Neison et al. 1900:46.
11. Cramer 1811:40.
12. Cramer 1811:39–40.
13. Schwegman 2001.
14. 1964:118.
15. Schwegman 2001.
16. Stone 1974:175–176.
17. Cotterell 1963:324.
18. 1963:282.
19. Cotterell 1963:49.
20. Ketchum 1991:32.
21. 1991:30.

22. Jones and Sullivan 1985:79, 88.
23. Neumann and Kravic 1975:47, Figure 19.
24. 1970:63.
25. Wilson 1981:19.
26. Wagner and McCorvie 1992:Figure 9.20A.
27. Smith 1993:212.
28. 1981:94.
29. Neumann and 1975:30–31.
30. 1975:176.
31. Schwegman 2001.
32. Richardson 1940:14.
33. Edwards and Wells 1993:30.
34. Wagner 2003:Appendix B.
35. Hilliam 1987; and Baillie 1985.
36. Hilliam 1987:141.
37. Hilliam 1987:149.

6. How They Did It: Building the America

1. Greenhill 1995.
2. Carmony 1964; Phillips 1947; Botkin 1955.
3. Botkin 1955; Brush 1944; Carmony 1964; Phillips 1947.
4. Carmony 1964.
5. Schwegman 2001:22.

7. The Wreck of the America

1. Botkin 1955:311; Brush 1944:50; Phillips 1947:21.
2. Brooks 1968:158–159.
3. Young 1981:35.
4. Brush 1944:155.
5. Young 1981:136.
6. Wagner and McCorvie 2006:219–247.
7. Cumings 1832, emphasis added.
8. Cumings 1838, emphasis added.
9. Cramer 1811, 1814.
10. Cramer 1811:33–34.
11. Jackson 1978:122.
12. Jackson 1978:125.

Bibliography

Allen, Michael
    1991 The Ohio River: Artery of Movement. In *Always a River*, edited by Robert L. Reid, pp. 105–129. Indiana University Press, Bloomington.
    1990 *Western Rivermen, 1763–1861.* Louisiana State University Press, Baton Rouge.
Alvord, Clarence W, and Clarence Edwin Carter (editors)
    1921 *Trade and Politics, 1767–1769.* Collections of the Illinois State Historical Library Vol. 16. British Series Vol 3. Illinois State Historical Library, Springfield.
Ambler, Charles Henry
    1932 *A History of Transportation in the Ohio Valley.* Arthur H. Clark, Glendale, California.
Anderson, Richard K.
    1995 *Guidelines for Recording Historic Ships.* National Park Service, Washington, D.C.
Anonymous
    1806 The Journal of a Trip from Champaign County, Ohio, and down the Mississippi River to New Orleans with a Cargo of Flour, 25 Nov. 1805–26 July 1806. Manuscript Collection SC2148, Illinois State Historical Library, Springfield.
    1943 News and Comment. *Journal of the Illinois State Historical Society* 36:422–424.
Baillie, M. G. L.
    1985 *A Slice through Time.* B. T. Batsford, London.
Baker, Mark
    1998 *Sons of a Trackless Forest.* Baker's Trace, Franklin, Tennessee.
Baldwin, Leland
    1941 *The Keelboat Age on Western Waters.* University of Pittsburgh Press.

Bancroft, Mark
1835   Mark Lee's Narrative. *Casket* 7:301–310.
Bedford, Dr. John R.
1919   A Tour in 1807 down the Cumberland, Ohio, and Mississippi Rivers from Nashville to New Orleans. *Tennessee Historical Magazine* 5:41–68.
Blair, Walter, and Franklin J. Meine (editors)
1956   *Half Horse, Half Alligator.* University of Chicago Press, Chicago.
Bonnemains, Jacqueline
1984   Charles-Alexandre Lesueur en Amerique du Nord (1816–1827). *Annales du Museum du Havre,* dossier 41, no. 30 (May 1984).
Botkin, B. A.
1955   *A Treasury of Mississippi River Folklore.* Crown, New York.
Bradbury, John
1819   *Travels in the Interior of North America, in the Years 1809, 1810, and 1811.* Sherwood, Neely, and Jones, London.
Brush, Daniel Harmon
1944   *Growing Up with Southern Illinois.* R. R. Donnelley, Chicago.
Bryant, William C.
1872   *Picturesque America.* D. Appleton, New York.
Caldwell, Norman
1950   Fort Massac: The American Frontier Post, 1778–1806. *Journal of the Illinois State Historical Society* 43:265–281.
Carmony, Donald D. F.
1964   Flatboat Building on Little Raccoon Creek, Parke County, Indiana. *Indiana Magazine of History* 60(4):305–322.
Carson, B. Coleman
1920   Transportation and Traffic on the Ohio and Mississippi before the Steamboat. *Mississippi Valley Historical Review* 7:1:26–38.
Claiborne, J. F. H.
1880   *Mississippi as a Province, Territory, and State.* Power and Bakesdale, Jackson, Mississippi.
Cockrum, William M.
1907   *A Pioneer History of Indiana.* Press of Oakland City Journal, Oakland City, Indiana.
Collot, Georges-Henri-Victor
1826   *Voyage dans L'Amerique Septentrionale.* Paris.
Corning, Howard (editor)
1929   Journal of John James Audubon. Business Historical Society, Cambridge, Massachusetts.

Cotterell, Howard Herschel

1963 *Old Pewter, Its Makers and Marks in England, Scotland, and Ireland.* Charles E. Tuttle, Rutland, Vermont.

Cramer, Zadok

1811 *The Navigator.* 7th ed. Cramer, Spear, and Eichbaum, Pittsburgh.

Cumings, Samuel

1838 *The Western Pilot.* N. and G. Guilford, Cincinnati.

1832 *The Western Pilot.* N. and G. Guilford, Cincinnati.

Deiss, Ron

1981 *The Development and Application of a Chronology for American Glass.* Midwestern Archaeological Research Center, Illinois State University, Bloomington.

Dunbar, Seymour

1915 *A History of Travel in America.* Vol. 1. Bobbs-Merrill, Indianapolis.

Edwards, Jay D., and Tom Wells

1993 *Historic Louisiana Nails.* The Fred B. Kniffen Cultural Resources Laboratory Monograph Series No. 2. Geoscience Publications, Department of Geography and Anthropology, Louisiana State University, Baton Rouge.

Ellicott, Andrew

1803 *The Journal of Andrew Ellicott.* Budd and Bartram, Philadelphia.

Flint, Timothy

1830a Col. Plug. *Western Monthly Magazine* 354–359.

1830b The Boat-Wreckers, Or Banditti of the West. *Casket* 3:103–106.

1968 *Recollections of the Last Ten Years in the Valley of the Mississippi,* edited by George E. Brooks. Southern Illinois University Press, Carbondale.

Forman, Major Samuel

1888 *Narrative of a Journey down the Ohio and Mississippi Rivers in 1789–1790,* compiled by Lyman Draper. Robert Clarke, Cincinnati.

Greenhill, Basil

1976 *Archaeology of the Boat.* Wesleyan University Press, Middletown, Connecticut.

1995 *The Archaeology of Boats and Ships: An Introduction.* Naval Institute Press, Annapolis, Maryland.

Hamilton, Thomas

1833 *Men and Manners in America.* Edinburgh, Scotland.

Hamy, Ernest-Theodore

1968 *The Travels of the French Naturalist Charles A. Lesueur in North America.* Kent State University Press, Kent, Ohio.

Havinghurst, Walter
1964 *Voices on the River.* Macmillan, New York.

Hilliam, J.
1987 Problems of Dating and Interpreting Results from Archaeological Timbers. In *Applications of Tree-Ring Studies,* edited by R. G. W. Ward, pp. 141–155. BAR International Series 333, Oxford, England.

Hulbert, Archer B.
1920 *The Paths of Inland Commerce.* Yale University Press, New Haven.

Jackson, Donald (editor)
1978 *Letters of the Lewis and Clark Expedition.* University of Illinois Press, Urbana.

Johnson, Leland
1980 The Doyle Mission to Massac, 1794. *Journal of the Illinois State Historical Society* 73:1:2–16.

Jones, Olive, and Catherine Sullivan
1985 *The Parks Canada Glass Glossary for the Description of Containers, Tableware, Closures, and Flat Glass.* National Historic Parks and Sites, Canadian Parks Service, Environment Canada.

Kauffman, Henry J.
1972 *American Axes: A Survey of Their Development and Their Makers.* Stephen Greene Press, Brattleboro, Vermont.

Ketchum, William C.
1991 *American Redware.* Henry Holt, New York.

Krisman, Kevin J.
1993 An Archaeological Approach. In *Boats: A Manual for Their Documentation,* edited by Paul Lipke, Peter Spectre, and Benjamin A. G. Fuller. American Association for State and Local History, Nashville.

Langsner, Drew
1978 *Country Woodcraft.* Rodale Press, Emmaus, Pennsylvania.

Lewis, Henry
1967 *The Valley of the Mississippi Illustrated.* Minnesota Historical Society, St. Paul.

Lincoln, Abraham
1953 Biographical Sketch Written for John L. Scripps. In *The Collected Works of Abraham Lincoln,* Vol. 4, edited by Roy P. Basler, pp. 60–63. H. Wolff, New York.

Munsey, Cecil
1970 *The Illustrated Guide to Collecting Bottles.* Hawthorn Books, New York.

Navy Department
1941 *Nomenclature of Naval Vessels.* Prepared by the Division of Personnel Supervision and Management with the Cooperation of the Bureau of Ships, Washington, D.C.

Neison, Adrian, Dixon Kemp, and C. Christopher Davies.
1900 *Practical Boat Building and Sailing.* L. Upcott Gill, London.

Neumann, George C., and Frank J. Kravic
1975 *Collector's Illustrated Guide of the American Revolution.* Rebel, Texarkana, Texas.

Newell, Mark
1996 *The Historic Working Small Craft of South Carolina.* Ph.D. dissertation, University of St. Andrews, Laurinburg, North Carolina.

Nuttall, Thomas
1819 *A Journal of Travels in the Arkansas Territory.* Thomas W. Palmer, Philadelphia.

Peck, John Mason
1834 *A Gazetteer of Illinois in Three Parts.* R. Goudy, Jacksonville, Illinois.

Perrin, William Henry
1883 *History of Alexander, Union, and Pulaski Counties, Illinois.* O. L. Baskin, Chicago.

Phillips, Josephine E.
1947 *Flatboating on the Great Thoroughfare.* Bulletin 1, Vol. 5:10–24. The Society, Cincinnati.

Prigge, Daniel
1973 *History of the Mouth of the Cache River.* Prepared for Mound City, Illinois, through funding provided by the Department of Local Government Affairs.

Records, T. W.
1946 Flatboats. *Indiana Magazine of History* 43:4:323–342.

Reid, Robert L., and Dan Hughes Fuller
1997 *Pilgrims on the Ohio.* Indiana Historical Society, Indianapolis.

Richardson, William
1940 *Journal from Boston to the Western Country and down the Ohio and Mississippi Rivers to New Orleans.* Valve Pilot Corporation, New York.

Rodney, Thomas
1997 *A Journey through the West: Thomas Rodney's 1803 journal from Delaware to the Mississippi Territory,* edited by Dwight L. Smith and Ray Swick. Ohio University Press, Athens.

Rothert, Otto
1924 *The Outlaws of Cave-in-Rock.* A. H. Clark, Cleveland.

Salaman, R. A.
   1977 *Dictionary of Tools Used in the Woodworking and Allied Trades, c. 1700–1970.* Charles Scribner's Sons, New York.
Scheiber, Harry N.
   1969 The Ohio-Mississippi Flatboat Trade: Some Reconsiderations. In *The Frontier in American Development,* edited by David M. Ellis, pp. 277–299. Cornell University Press, Ithaca.
Schwegman, John
   2001 Ohio River Flatboat. *Springhouse* 2:23–25.
Schultz, Christian
   1810 *Travels on an Inland Voyage.* Isaac Riley, New York.
Sellens, Alvin
   2002 *Dictionary of American Hand Tools.* Schiffer, Atglen, Pennsylvania.
Shapiro, Michael Edward, Barbara Groseclose, Elizabeth Johns, Paul C. Nagel, and John Wilmerding
   1990 *George Caleb Bingham.* Harry N. Abrams, New York.
Sloane, Eric
   1982 *Eric Sloane's America.* Promontory Press, New York.
Smith, Samuel (editor)
   1993 *Fort Southwest Archaeological Site: A Multidisciplinary Interpretation.* Research Series No. 9. Tennessee Department of Environment and Conservation, Division of Archaeology, Nashville.
South, Stanley
   1964 Analysis of the Buttons from Brunswick Town and Fort Fisher. *Florida Anthropologist* 17(2):113–133.
Stevens, James P.
   1976 Last Days of the Ship Caulking Trade. In *Wooden Shipbuilding and Small Craft Preservation,* pp. 93–96. National Trust for Historic Preservation, Washington, D.C.
Stone, Lyle
   1974 *Fort Michilimackinac, 1715–1781.* Publications of the Museum, Michigan State Anthropological Series, Vol. 2. East Lansing, Michigan.
Tabart and Company
   1807 *The Book of Trades, or Library of Useful Arts.* C. Squire, London.
Thorpe, T. B.
   1845 *The Mysteries of the Backwoods.* Carey and Hart, Philadelphia.
Thwaites, Reuben Gold
   1900 *Afloat on the Ohio.* Doubleday and McClure, New York.
Twain, Mark
   1896 *Life on the Mississippi.* Harper and Brothers, New York.

Wagner, Mark J.

    2003 *The Flatboat America (11Pu280): An Early Nineteenth Century Ohio River Flatboat Wreck in Pulaski, Illinois.* Technical Report 03-1. Center for Archaeological Investigations, Southern Illinois University Carbondale, Carbondale, Illinois.

Wagner, Mark J., and Brian M. Butler

    1999 *Archaeological Investigations at the Rose Hotel (11Hn-116), Hardin County, Illinois.* Technical Report 99–3. Center for Archaeological Investigations, Southern Illinois University Carbondale, Carbondale, Illinois.

Wagner, Mark J., and Mary R. McCorvie

    2011 The Pirates of Cave-in-Rock in Myth and Legend. *Springhouse Magazine* 28(1):9–14.

    2006 Going to See the Varmint: Piracy in Myth and Reality on the Ohio and Mississippi Rivers, 1785–1830. In *The Archaeology of Piracy*, edited by Charles R. Ewen and Russell Skowronek, pp. 219–247 (with Mary R. McCorvie). University of Florida Press, Gainesville.

    1992 *The Old Landmark.* Center for American Archaeology, Kampsville, Illinois.

White, Richard

    1991 *The Middle Ground.* Cambridge University Press, Cambridge.

Wilson, Rex

    1981 *Bottles on the Western Frontier.* University of Arizona Press, Tucson.

Young, Chester Raymond (editor)

    1981 *Westward into Kentucky: The Narrative of Daniel Trabue.* University Press of Kentucky, Lexington.

Mark J. Wagner is the director of the Center for Archaeological Investigations, Southern Illinois University Carbondale. He is a former president of the Illinois Archaeological Survey and the author of *The Rhoads Site: A Historic Kickapoo Village on the Illinois Prairie,* as well as numerous essays, technical reports, and books.